Industrial Strength C++

 **Prentice Hall Series in Innovative Technology**

Dennis R. Allison, David J. Farber, and Bruce D. Shriver   *Series Advisors*

Industrial Strength C++
Rules and Recommendations

Mats Henricson

Erik Nyquist

To join a Prentice Hall PTR mailing list, point to:
http://www.prenhall.com/register

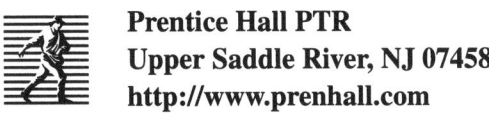

Prentice Hall PTR
Upper Saddle River, NJ 07458
http://www.prenhall.com

Library of Congress Cataloging-in-Publication Data

Henricson, Mats, 1963-
    Industrial strength C++ / Mats Henricson, Erik Nyquist.
      p. cm.
    Includes index.
    ISBN 0-13-120965-5 (paper)
    1. C++ (Computer program language)   I. Nyquist, Erik, 1964-
II. Title
    QA76.73.C153H46   1996
    005.13'3--dc21   96-44404
                                                    CIP

Editorial Production: *Precision Graphic Services, Inc.*
Acquisitions Editor: *Paul W. Becker*
Manufacturing Manager: *Alexis R. Heydt*
Cover Design Director: *Jerry Votta*
Cover Design: *Wanda Lubelska*

 Published by Prentice Hall PTR
Prentice-Hall, Inc.
A Simon & Schuster Company
Upper Saddle River, NJ 07458

The publisher offers discounts on this book when ordered
in bulk quantities. For more information, contact:

            Corporate Sales Department
            Prentice Hall PTR
            1 Lake Street
            Upper Saddle River, NJ 07458
            Phone: 800-382-3419
            FAX: 201-236-7141
            E-mail: corpsales@prenhall.com

Printed in the United States of America
10 9 8 7 6 5 4 3 2 1

ISBN 0-13-120965-5

Prentice-Hall International (UK) Limited, *London*
Prentice-Hall of Australia Pty. Limited, *Sydney*
Prentice-Hall Canada, Inc., *Toronto*
Prentice-Hall Hispanoamericana S.A., *Mexico*
Prentice-Hall of India Private Limited, *New Delhi*
Prentice-Hall of Japan, Inc., *Tokyo*
Simon & Schuster Asia Pte. Ltd., *Singapore*
Editora Prentice-Hall do Brasil, Ltda., *Rio de Janeiro*

Contents

Examples

Acknowledgments

We would like to thank Paul Becker, our editor, for believing in seemingly imaginary progress from Sweden. Without his support, year after year, this book would never have been finished. Next in line are the people at Precision Graphics that helped us to turn the manuscript into a book, especially Kirsten Dennison. We would also like to thank Scott Meyers for reading a very rough first version of the book and giving us the comments it deserved. Other reviewers whom we would like to give special thanks to are Sean Corfield, who has enlightened us numerous times from his vast knowledge of both C and C++, Kevlin A. P. Henney for tons and tons of excellent comments, and Geoff Kuenning for his patient corrections of our shaky handling of the weird language called English. Other reviewers we would like to thank are, in no particular order, Dean Quanne, Peter Dickson, Per Andersson, Les Hatton, Johan Bengtsson, John Kewley, Karl Dickson, Justin Forder, Stefan Frennemo, Mats Lidell, Eric Turesson, Peter Cederqvist, Michael Olsson, Björn Strihagen, Ulf Santesson, Roger Persson, Sven Tapper, Lars Petrus, and Staffan Blau. Please forgive us if we have forgotten anyone!

Special thanks from Mats: I would also like to thank Ellemtel Telecommunications Systems Labs, Ericsson, and PostNet for their support in the development of the book. Last but not least, I would like to thank Åsa for her patience and support.

Special thanks from Erik: I would also like to thank Ericsson Radio Messaging, ENEA Data, and Svenska Handelsbanken for their support in the development of the book. Most of all, I would like to thank Ulrika for her patience and support.

Preface

This book defines a C++ coding standard that should be valid and usable for almost all programmers. ISO 9000 and the Capability Maturity Model (CMM) state that coding standards are mandatory for any company with quality ambitions. However, developing such a coding standard is a nontrivial task, particularly for a complex multiparadigm language such as C++. In this book we give you a good start toward a programming standard for your company or project. Such standards are often written by the most experienced programmers in a company. If a quality manager responsible for the development of such a standard instead selects this book as the base, experienced programmers can be relieved of this arduous task and instead continue to do what they prefer to do: design the company's products. This book should also be of great interest to C++ programmers trying to find ways of improving their code.

Since 1992, when our public-domain Ellemtel C++ coding standard was released, we have greatly expanded our knowledge with insights from many years of C++ development in multi-million-dollar projects, as well as inside knowledge of what is going on in the standardization of C++. We have carefully selected and concisely formulated the guidelines we believe are really important, and divided them into rules and recommendations, based on how important it is to follow the standard. Thus, we give novices good advice without restraining experts from using the full power of the language. Most of these rules and recommendations are written so that it should be possible to check with a tool whether they are broken. Text and code examples explain each individual rule and recommendation.

Introduction

In early 1990, C++ was chosen as the implementation language for a huge telecommunications project at Ellemtel Telecommunications Systems Laboratories in Stockholm, Sweden. Erik wrote a programming standard for the project, a document that was later maintained by the two of us, working as the C++ support group. Then, in 1991, there was a discussion about programming standards in the newsgroup comp.lang.c++. Mats wrote a message describing the structure of our document. Suddenly we received an e-mail from Bjarne Stroustrup, the initial inventor of C++, asking if he could have a look at the document. The fact that it was written in Swedish was no problem to him, because he was born in Denmark, and Danish is fairly close to Swedish. The document was initially meant only for internal use, but shortly after Bjarne's e-mail we convinced our managers that it would be a good idea to make the document available to the public. By doing that we could use the Internet to review and improve our rules and recommendations. A few months later the document was translated into English and made available for anonymous FTP.

This document is now in use at many hundreds of companies, research centers and universities all over the world, from Chile and India to France, Australia, and the United States. However, it was written a long time ago. C++ has changed in many ways since 1992. Many new features have been added to the language, such as runtime type identification and namespaces, as well as a very powerful standard template library, but C++ is now stable and very close to becoming an international standard. The way C++ is used has changed a lot. What was previously looked on with suspicion, such as multiple inheritance, is now accepted. With this as background it is time for a major revision of the C++ rules and recommendations document, now as a book from Prentice Hall.

What we have done is to rewrite our rules and recommendations document from scratch while preserving the structure that made it so popular.

Programming standards must be valid both for newcomers and experts. This is sometimes very difficult to accomplish. We have solved this problem by differentiating our guidelines into rules and recommendations. Rules should almost never be broken by anyone, whereas recommendations are supposed to be followed most of the time, unless there is a good reason not to. This division allows experts to break a recommendation, or even sometimes a rule, if they badly need to.

We are explicitly listing all rules and recommendations, instead of having them somewhere in a block of text, entangled within discussions and code examples. We have been very careful to find the shortest and most accurate formulation possible. We also try to give helpful alternatives instead of just warning the reader about dangerous practices.

The book consists of 15 chapters and two appendices, each discussing a particular aspect of C++ programming.

Chapter 1 is about naming. We discuss how names of classes and functions should be chosen, written, and administrated to make programs easy to understand, read, and maintain.

Chapter 2 is about the organization of code. We discuss how code should be organized in files.

Chapter 3 discusses how comments should be used to add whatever information a company, organization, or individual needs. Well written comments are often the sign of a good programmer.

Chapter 4 is about control flow statements, such as `for`, `while`, `switch`, and `if`. If used improperly, they can increase the complexity of a program.

Chapter 5 is a long chapter about the life cycle of objects. We discuss how objects are best declared, created, initialized, copied, assigned, and destroyed.

Chapter 6 discusses conversions. We suggest a few rules and recommendations that can take some of the dangers out of this tricky part of C++.

Chapter 7 is a long chapter concerning the class interface. Among the topics discussed are inline functions, argument passing and return values, `const`, operator and function overloading, default arguments, and conversion operators.

Chapter 8 discusses how best to use `new` and `delete`.

Chapter 9 discusses problems related to static objects, such as global objects, static data members, file scope objects and local variables declared static.

Chapter 10 is also a long chapter, because it discusses fundamental parts of object oriented programming, namely encapsulation, dynamic binding, inheritance, and software contracts.

Chapter 11 is a short chapter about assertions.

Chapter 12 is long because it discusses error handling, particularly exception handling. Rules and recommendations cover when exceptions should be thrown, what kind of objects you should throw, how you can recover from errors, how to make your code exception safe, and how exceptions are best documented.

Chapter 13 explains what parts of C++ you should avoid. Some parts of the language and the standard library are so error prone that they should be avoided.

Chapter 14 is about the size of executables, that is, how program size often can be traded for performance, and vice versa.

Chapter 15 is a large chapter devoted entirely to the issue of portability. Questions we discuss include how nonportable code should be handled, how files should be included, how to avoid depending on the size or layout of objects, and how you best avoid features not supported by some compilers.

Appendix A discusses programming style. Style issues can often start heated debates, which is why we put all this into an appendix instead of making it a normal chapter. We discuss, among other things, naming conventions and lexical style. Appendix B is a glossary.

We believe this book presents the best C++ programming standard you can get, but of course it is not enough. You also need experienced system architects and programmers well aware of different design practices, as well as the problem domain in which your company exists. Such knowledge is generally not C++-specific and is therefore beyond the scope of this book. Other areas not discussed in this book are testing, metrics, procedures for code reviews, and prototyping, or how to transform requirements into design ideas (object-oriented analysis and design). We concentrate on C++ specific issues that will improve the quality of your code.

We assume the reader knows the basics of C++. If you need an introduction to C++, we recommend the following books:

- Bjarne Stroustrup. *The C++ Programming Language,* Second Edition. Addison-Wesley, 1991. ISBN 0-201-53992-6.
- Marshall P. Cline and Greg A. Lomow. *C++ FAQs.* Addison Wesley, 1995. ISBN 0-201-58958-3.
- Robert B. Murray. *C++ Strategies and Tactics.* Addison Wesley, 1993. ISBN 0-201-56382-7.

For the latest details on the language definition, we have used this document:

- *Working Paper for Draft Proposed International Standard for Information Systems—Programming Language C++.*

The document with this extraordinary long title (often called just the "Working Paper") defines the current status of the proposed C++ standard. A new version of the "Working Paper" comes every four months, but it is usually accessible only to people involved in the standardization of C++. Therefore, if you would like to look at some of the inner details of C++, we recommend this highly interesting book:

- Bjarne Stroustrup. *The Design and Evolution of C++.* Addison-Wesley, 1994. ISBN 0-201-54330-3.

All code examples in this book try to follow the "Working Paper" description of C++. Except when explicitly stated differently, code should also follow the rules and recommendations described in this book.

You are encouraged to contact us with questions and comments at rules@henricson.se

Erik Nyquist and Mats Henricson
Stockholm, June 1996

chapter one

Naming

If you do not choose, write, and administer names with care, you will end up with a program that is hard to understand, read, and maintain.

Meaningful Names

Names must be chosen with care. It is unlikely that a class or function will be used more than once if the user does not understand the names or the abstractions they represent. Good abstractions are essential for low maintenance costs, a high level of reuse, and traceability from requirements to program code.

RULES AND RECOMMENDATIONS

Rec. 1.1   Use meaningful names.

Rec. 1.2   Use English names for identifiers.

Rec. 1.3   Be consistent when naming functions, types, variables, and constants.

See Also

Rule 1.8–Rule 1.9: Some identifiers are not legal.

Rec. 3.5: All comments should be written in English

Style A.2–Style A.8: How identifiers should be written.

Rec. 1.1 Use meaningful names. Classes, typedefs, functions, variables, namespaces, and files are all given names. Suitable names are meaningful to the person using the abstractions provided, and do not change if

- The implementation changes.
- A program is ported to another environment.
- Source code is used in a new context.

Abbreviations are not always meaningful and can be difficult to understand. It is best to avoid abbreviations as much as possible. Use only commonly accepted abbreviations (such as IBM).

EXAMPLE 1.1 **Naming a variable**

```
int strL;          // Not recommended
int stringLength;  // Recommended
```

Rec. 1.2 Use English names for identifiers. Do not use names that are difficult to understand. Most importantly, do not use names that are understood only by those who understand your native language. What does the word *Bil* mean to an English or Japanese programmer? Not many know that it is the Swedish word for *car*.

Rec. 1.3 Be consistent when naming functions, types, variables, and constants. Consistent names for member functions make it possible to reuse both code and existing knowledge. If function names are consistent, the user of a class will have to know less about the class and will find it easier to use.

EXAMPLE 1.2 **Different ways to print an object**

Many objects are printed by using the << operator (left-shift) with an ostream and the object as arguments.

```
ostream& operator<<(ostream&, const EmcString&);

EmcString s("printing");
cout << s << endl;
```

Other classes also provide member functions for the same purpose.

```
class EmcFruit
{
   public:
      // ...
      virtual ostream& print(ostream&) const = 0;
};

class EmcApple : public EmcFruit
{
   public:
      // ...
      virtual ostream& print(ostream&) const;
};
```

Such member functions are often `virtual` and are meant only to be called indirectly by the base class implementation.

```
// Works for all classes derived from EmcFruit

inline ostream& operator<<(ostream& s, const EmcFruit& f)
{
   return f.print(s); // calls virtual member function
}
```

Because the virtual functions are not used directly, the code will be more readable because objects of different classes are printed the same way.

```
EmcFruit* fp = new EmcApple;

cout << *fp << endl;
```

EXAMPLE 1.3 **Naming accessors and modifiers**

Some naming conventions are more indirect; for example, if a class has a member function that returns a value, how should a member function that modifies the value be named?

In general it is a bad idea to always provide a corresponding modifier, but if one is provided, it should have the same name as the corresponding accessor.

For example, the class `Point` has two data members, xM and yM, with appropriate accessors and modifiers as shown below.

```
Point p(0,0);          // a point in a 2-dimensional space
p.x(1);                // set X-coordinate
cout << p.x() << endl; // prints X-coordinate, "1"
```

There are many more such naming conventions, some of which are covered in Appendix A at the end of this book. Style rules are optional, not mandatory. Each organization may have its own set of preferences. Choose one style and stick to it, and make certain that the recommendations are followed.

EXAMPLE 1.4   **Names used by a template function**

If templates are used in your application, consistent naming makes it possible to use the same source code for a number of unrelated but similar data types. Many good examples are found in the standard template library for C++.

The following template function can be used with any array type that has an indexing operator, a `size()` member function, and a type `Index`, defined such that objects of the type `T` can be assigned to the return value of the indexing operator. This is an example of the benefits of consistent naming.

```
// typename to mark a qualified name as a type name.

template <class Array, class T>
void check_assign(Array& a, typename Array::Index i, T t)
{
    if (i < a.size())
    {
        a[i] = t;
    }
}
```

The qualifier `typename` is a recent addition to the language. When a name is qualified with a template parameter, the name is by default treated as the name of a member and the qualifier `typename` must be used for all names that are type names.

Names That Collide

There are many global names in a C++ program. Before the introduction of namespaces it was sometimes difficult to avoid identical identifiers in the global scope, particularly when several class libraries were combined.

A related issue is how to prevent the names of macros and files from colliding.

RULES AND	Rec. 1.4	Only `namespace` **names should be global.**
RECOMMENDATIONS	Rec. 1.5	**Do not use global** `using` **declarations and** `using` **directives inside header files.**
	Rec. 1.6	**Prefixes should be used to group macros.**
	Rec. 1.7	**Group related files by using a common prefix in the file name.**

See Also   Rec. 15.5–Rec. 15.6: How to include header files.

Rec. 15.13: If namespaces are not supported by your compiler.

Rec. 1.4 Only namespace names should be global.

A name clash occurs when a name is defined in more than one place. For example, two different class libraries could give two different classes the same name. If you try to use many class libraries at the same time, there is a fair chance that you will be unable to compile or link the program because of name clashes.

We recommend that you have as few names as possible in the global scope. In C++ this means that names that would otherwise be global should be declared and defined inside namespaces.

It is no longer necessary to have global types, variables, constants, and functions if namespaces are supported by your compiler. Names inside namespaces are as easy to use as global names, except that you sometimes must use the scope operator.

Without namespaces it is common to add a common identifier as a prefix to the name of each class in a set of related classes. A common identifier is usually a combination of two to six letters.

We have chosen to use prefixes when writing our examples for this book because namespaces are a new feature not yet supported by all compilers.

EXAMPLE 1.5   Namespace

A namespace is a declarative region in which classes, functions, types, and templates can be defined.

```
namespace Emc
{
    class String { ... };
    // ...
}
```

A namespace is open, which means that new names can be added to an existing namespace.

```
// previous definition of Emc exists

namespace Emc
{
    template <class T>
    class DynamicArray
    {
      // ...
    };
}
```

EXAMPLE 1.6   Accessing names from namespace

A name qualified with a namespace name refers to a member of the namespace.

```
Emc::String s;
```

A `using` declaration makes it possible to use a name from a namespace without the scope operator.

```
using Emc::String;        // using declaration
String s1;
```

It is possible to make all names from a namespace accessible with a `using` directive.

```
using namespace Emc;      // using directive
String s;                 // Emc::String s;
Array<String> a;          // Emc::Array<Emc::String> a;
```

EXAMPLE 1.7   Class as namespace

Syntactically, namespaces are similar to classes, because declarations and definitions can also be nested inside classes. Semantically, there are a few differences, however, and some of them are worth pointing out.

If a declaration or definition of a function is put inside a name space, only the global name of the function changes. On the other hand, if you put a function declaration inside a class, it becomes a member function that can be called only with an object. A member function must be declared `static` in order to make it possible to call it as a free function.

If a function definition is put inside a class, the function automatically becomes inline. A global function or a function inside a namespace must be explicitly declared `inline`.

Classes are sometimes used as namespaces, though. The recommendation is that the static member functions and nested types should be strongly related to the class to which they belong.

EXAMPLE 1.8 **Class names with prefixes**

```
EmcString s1;    // Belongs to the Emc class library
OtherString s2;  // Belongs to the Other class library
```

Rec. 1.5 Do not use global `using` declarations and `using` directives inside header files.

A `using` declaration or a `using` directive in the global scope in header files is not recommended because it will make names globally accessible to all files that include that header, which is what we are trying to avoid.

Inside an implementation file, `using` declarations and `using` directives are less dangerous and sometimes very convenient.

On the other hand, too-frequent use of the scope operator is not recommended. The difference between local names and other names is more explicit, but more code must be rewritten if the namespaces are reorganized.

Rec. 1.6 Prefixes should be used to group macros.

There are no namespaces for file names and macros because these are part of the language environment, rather than the language. Such names should therefore always include a common identifier as a prefix.

Rec. 1.7 Group related files by using a common prefix in the file name.

For file names there is one important exception. If the common identifier makes the file name too long for the operating system to handle, it may be necessary to use directories to group files. This is often the case when writing code for DOS or Microsoft Windows.

EXAMPLE 1.9 **Names of include files**

```
#include "RWCstring.h"      /* Recommended */
#include "rw/cstring.h"      /* Sometimes needed */
```

Illegal Naming

It does not matter which naming convention you use, as long as it is consistent. But there are actually a few kinds of names that are rather confusing, or plain wrong. Such names should be avoided in all naming conventions.

RULES AND RECOMMENDATIONS

Rule 1.8 Do not use identifiers that contain two or more underscores in a row.

Rule 1.9 Do not use identifiers that begin with an underscore.

See Also Style A.2–Style A.5: Names of identifiers.

Rule 1.8 Do not use identifiers that contain two or more underscores in a row.

Rule 1.9 Do not use identifiers that begin with an underscore.

Identifiers containing a double underscore (__) or beginning with an underscore and an uppercase letter are reserved by the compiler, and should therefore not be used by programmers. To be on the safe side it is best to avoid the use of all identifiers beginning with an underscore.

EXAMPLE 1.10 **Use of underscores in names**

```
const int i__j = 11;    // Illegal
const int _K = 22;      // Illegal
const int _m = 33;      // Not recommended
```

Organizing the Code

Code is most often stored in files, even though some development environments also have other, more efficient representations as an alternative (such as precompiled headers). Guidelines for organizing the code in files are needed to make the code easy to compile.

RULES AND RECOMMENDATIONS

Rule 2.1	Each header file should be self-contained.
Rule 2.2	Avoid unnecessary inclusion.
Rule 2.3	Enclose all code in header files within `include` guards.
Rec. 2.4	Definitions for inline member functions should be placed in a separate file.
Rec. 2.5	Definitions for all template functions of a class should be placed in a separate file.

See Also

Style A.6–Style A.7: How include guards are written.

Style A.9–Style A.10: How file names are chosen.

Style A.15: Where inline functions are defined.

Rule 2.1 Each header file should be self-contained. The purpose of a header file is to group type definitions, declarations, and macros. It should be self-contained so that nothing more than the inclusion of a single header file is needed to use the full interface of a class. A rather common error is to forget to include a necessary header file. This could happen, for example, when a header file has not been tested in isolation. By pure coincidence, the forgotten file is included by another file. One way to test your header file is to always include it first in the corresponding implementation files. For this to work, the header file must be self-contained.

EXAMPLE 2.1 **Testing for self-containment**

```
// EmcArray.cc

#include "EmcArray.hh"
#include <iostream.h>
// ...

// The rest of the EmcArray.cc file
```

Rule 2.2 Avoid unnecessary inclusion. The opposite, too much inclusion, is even more common. Very often a file is included more than once because it is required to make different header files self-contained. It is also common that a file is included even though it is not needed at all.

Before an object can be created, its size must be known and that size can be found only by inspecting the class definition. If an object of the class is used as return value, argument, data member, or variable with static storage duration, the header file containing the class definition must be included.

It should be enough to forward-declare a class if it is only referred to by pointer or reference in the header file. There are some important exceptions, however. The class definition must be included if a member function is called or a pointer is dereferenced. It should also be included if a pointer or reference is cast to another type.

Remember that the inclusion of a header file makes the implementation of inline member functions visible to the user. If the implementation of an inline member function operates on an object of a class, that class definition must be visible even though only pointers or references are used. The presence of inline member functions increases the number of files that must be recompiled when a class definition is modified. You can shorten your compile time by avoiding inline functions, but that will instead reduce the runtime performance of your program.

If an inline function contains casts between forward-declared types, no inclusion is needed, but such an implementation has a potential bug. If two classes are forward-declared and they are related through inheritance, a cast will not give the correct result if multiple inheritance is used and pointer adjustments are required. This is another case that requires the class definitions to be visible.

EXAMPLE 2.2   **Data member of class type**

```
#include "A.hh"

class X
{
   public:
      A    returnA();              // A.hh must be #included
      void withAParameter(A a);    // A.hh must be #included
   private:
      A    aM;                     // A.hh must be #included
};
```

EXAMPLE 2.3   **Forward declaration**

```
// Forward declaration

class B;

class Y
{
   public:
      B*   returnBPtr();
      void withConstBRefParameter(const B& b);
   private:
      B*   bM;
};
```

Rule 2.3 Enclose all code in header files within include guards.

Header files are often included many times in a program. A standard header such as string.h is a good example. Because C++ does not allow multiple definitions of a class, it is necessary to prevent the compiler from reading the definitions more than once. The standard technique, as well as the only portable one, is to use an include guard so that the source code is seen only the first time the compiler reads the file. By defining a macro inside a conditional preprocessor directive, which can be done only if the macro has not been defined, the preprocessor prevents the compiler from seeing the source code in a header file more than once.

It is important to have unique macros among the set of header files, or the compiler will see only one of the header files using the same macro name. If there are no files in your system with identical names, and you have a one-to-one correspondence between the macro name and the file name, this should not be a problem.

Writing and maintaining programs is much easier if there is a sensible mapping between the name of a file and its content. For example, nobody is going to like you if you put the `String` class in the file `Stack.hh`. The ideal is to have one file for each class because that makes it very easy to give the file a good name, but quite often this is not possible, especially if you are constrained to use very short file names by an operating system such as MS-DOS.

In such cases it is reasonable to put several class definitions in the same header file, but only if the classes are closely related. It is much easier to give a good name to a closely related collection of classes than one that is formed arbitrarily. More importantly there is less risk that classes are included without reason.

A classic example is a list class, which often provides a special iterator class for iteration over the list. Because the iterator is useless without the list, it is natural to put both the list class and the iterator class in the same file. An advantage of doing so is that the user will need to include only one file to use the list abstraction. With separate header files for each class, you need to find unique names for even more files, which can be difficult if you are constrained by an operating system such as MS-DOS.

EXAMPLE 2.4   `include` **guard**

```
#ifndef EMCQUEUE_HH
#define EMCQUEUE_HH


// Rest of header file


#endif
```

Rec. 2.4 Definitions for inline member functions should be placed in a separate file.

In Appendix A we recommend that all inline member functions should be defined outside of the class definition. If definitions of inline functions are outside the class, the class declaration will be much easier to read. The best place to put such inline functions is in a separate file: an inline definition file.

An inline definition file should normally be included by the corresponding header file. Sometimes frequent changes to inline definition files make the compilation times unnecessarily long, and if that is a problem, inline definition files are best included in the implementation file. It is necessarily to remove all `inline` keywords first; otherwise you will get link errors. With macros, such changes can be made without changing the source code.

EXAMPLE 2.5   **Disable inlining by using inline definition files**

EmcString.icc

```
#include <string.h>
// ...

// Do not include anything after this point

#ifdef DISABLE_INLINE
#define inline
#endif

// Definitions of inline functions

inline
const char* EmcString::cStr() const
{
    return cpM;
}

// ...

#ifdef DISABLE_INLINE
#undef inline
#endif
```

EmcString.hh

```
// Class declaration

// ...

// Always include at end

#ifndef DISABLE_INLINE
#include "EmcString.icc"
#endif
```

EmcString.cc

```
#include "EmcString.hh"

// Definitions of non-inline functions

// ...

// Always include at end

#ifdef DISABLE_INLINE
#include "EmcString.icc"
#endif
```

Rec. 2.5 Definitions for all template functions of a class should be placed in a separate file.

Templates are in one respect very similar to an inline function. No code is generated when the compiler sees the declaration of a template; code is generated only when a template instantiation is needed.

A function template instantiation is needed when the template is called or its address is taken; a class template instantiation is needed when an object of the template instantiation class is declared.

A big problem is that there is no standard for how code that uses templates is compiled. The compilers that require the complete template definition to be visible usually instantiate the template whenever it is needed and then use a flexible linker to remove redundant instantiations of the template member function. However, this solution is not possible on all systems; the linkers on most Unix-systems cannot do this.

This means that we have a potential portability problem when writing code that uses templates. We recommend that you put the implementation of template functions in a separate file, a template definition file, and use conditional compilation to control whether that file is included by the header file. A macro is either set or not depending on what compiler you use. An inconvenience is that you now have to manage more files.

There could also be a file with template functions that are declared `inline`. These should not be put in a template definition file.

EXAMPLE 2.6 **Function template**

```
template <class T>
T max(T x, T y)
{
    return (x > y) ? x : y;
}


void function(int i, int j)
{
    int m = max(i,j);  // must instantiate max(int,int)
    // ...
}
```

EXAMPLE 2.7 **Class template**

```
template <class T>
class EmcQueue
{
    public:
        EmcQueue();
        // ...
        void insert(const T& t);
};


EmcQueue<int> q;     // instantiate EmcQueue<int>
q.insert(42);        // instantiate EmcQueue<int>::insert
```

EXAMPLE 2.8 **Template header file**

EmcQueue.hh
```
template <class T>
class EmcQueue
{
    // ...
};


#ifndef DISABLE_INLINE
#include "EmcQueue.icc"
#endif


#ifndef EXTERNAL_TEMPLATE_DEFINITION
#include "EmcQueue.cc"
#endif
```

chapter three

Comments

A comment is an information carrier that makes it possible to add whatever information a company, organization, or individual needs. Comments are hard to maintain, so with a few exceptions they should explain only what is not obvious from reading the program itself.

If you have a standard format on all your comments, you can write tools to extract useful information from them. Such techniques are widespread in the industry, but currently there is no de facto standard format.

Well-written comments are the sign of a good programmer. Code without comments can be very hard to maintain, but too many comments can also be a hindrance. A good balance can be found by following a few simple recommendations.

RULES AND RECOMMENDATIONS

Rec. 3.1	Each file should contain a copyright comment.
Rec. 3.2	Each file should contain a comment with a short description of the file content.
Rec. 3.3	Every file should declare a local constant string that identifies the file.
Rec. 3.4	Use // for comments.
Rec. 3.5	All comments should be written in English.

See Also   Rec. 1.2: Use English for identifiers.

Rec. 1.4: How to define a local constant string in a namespace.

Rec. 10.7, Rec. 10.9: Documenting classes and templates.

Rec. 3.1 Each file should contain a copyright comment.   Many project teams copyright their code to prevent other companies or people from using it without permission. Sometimes a comment like this can be sufficient:

Short copyright comment

```
// Copyright <company> <years>. All Rights Reserved.
```

In some countries such comments may not be necessary to protect your code. However, it is a good idea to put such a comment into your code anyway. If nothing else, the copyright notice serves as a reminder, and it says where the code came from in the first place. It can sometimes also be useful to know who is the author(s) of a source file. Suppose you find a bug in some externally supplied code. Without a name or contacting address you cannot report this bug. The address is also necessary if you need to ask questions in order to understand a technical detail. Also, make sure that not just the original author but all programmers who have written and maintained the code are listed. In some cases the names of the authors are replaced by the address of a support organization that takes care of bug reports and questions.

The following comment has been used on many projects:

Long copyright comment

```
// Copyright <company> <years>. All Rights Reserved.
// <company address>
//
// The copyright to the computer program(s) herein
// is the property of <company>, <country>. The
// program(s) may be used and/or copied only with the
// written permission of <company> or in accordance
// with the terms and conditions stipulated in the
// agreement/contract under which the program(s) have
// been supplied. This copyright notice must not be
// removed.
```

Choose a style and stick to it. Long comments are harder to maintain, so unless there is a reason not to, use a one-line copyright comment, but first make sure the copyright text you intend to use is appropriate for the country where you work. Either consult the legal department at your company or contact a lawyer.

Copyright comments can be added automatically when the code is made available to a third party. This relieves the individual programmer of the need to keep these comments up to date with the company standard.

Rec. 3.2 Each file should contain a comment with a short description of the file content.

The best thing a programmer can do to avoid questions from other programmers is to write clear code, but a comment after the copyright comment with a short description of the file content can do wonders.

Comment describing the file content

```
// File Description:
// - <text>
//
// Authors: <name1> <address1>
//          <name2> <address2>
```

Rec. 3.3 Every file should declare a local constant string that identifies the file.

Comments are visible only in source files, so this information is not available if a class library is delivered without the source. Some information that otherwise would be in a comment is often provided in implementation files as static strings, which can easily be extracted by tools. Many version control programs, such as rcs and sccs, allow you to include variables in these static strings that are automatically expanded when the file is checked out. The version number is useful information when the client reports errors.

By using such version handling systems, you let the computer make sure comments are not outdated if someone else takes over the code for maintenance and forgets to update the list of authors.

EXAMPLE 3.1   **Static string identifying the file**

```
static const char rcsid[] = "$Id: $";
```

When using rcs, the variable $Id: $ is expanded with file name, version identity, date of last check-in, and the user identity of the person who last modified the file. If your compiler supports namespaces, you should consider removing the static keyword and have the definition inside an unnamed namespace.

Rec. 3.4 Use // for comments.

End-of-line comments are superior to /**/ comments. They are less difficult to remove, because they do not span multiple lines. This may be a weak argument compared to more personal aesthetic reasons, and hardened ex-C programmers may want to stay with what they learned originally, but /**/ comments do not nest. If /**/ comments are nested, the compiler will think that the whole comment ends after the first nested comment.

EXAMPLE 3.2   **Comments in C++**

```
char* cpM;      // A pointer to the characters
int  lenM;      /* The length of the character array */
```

EXAMPLE 3.3   **Nested** /**/ **comment**

```
/* No: this nested comment will not work !!!

char* cpM;      // A pointer to the characters
int  lenM;      /* The length of the character array */

*/
```

Rec. 3.5 All comments should be written in English.

All comments should be written in English, regardless of your native language. There are many reasons why:

- At large companies code may be shipped to another country for maintenance, and English is the language most likely to be understood by a randomly selected C++ programmer.
- You may think that the code will be viewed only by your group of programmers, but before you know it the sales department may have sold access to the source code to a customer.
- You may have to send the source code to your compiler supplier (or third-party library supplier) in order to allow them to hunt down bugs in their code (or to give you the support you have paid for). If they can read your comments, they may be able to help you faster.
- Comments written in other languages may be supported by the upcoming ISO C++ standard, but it will take quite some time before your compiler will support such comments because they contain characters outside the basic source character set.

chapter four

Control Flow

It is important to use control statements (`for`, `while`, `do-while`, `switch`, `case`, `if`, `else`, and `goto`) correctly and consistently so that they are easy to understand.

RULES AND RECOMMENDATIONS

Rule 4.1	Do not change a loop variable inside a `for` loop block.
Rec. 4.2	Update loop variables close to where the loop condition is specified.
Rec. 4.3	All flow control primitives (`if`, `else`, `while`, `for`, `do`, `switch`, and `case`) should be followed by a block, even if it is empty.
Rec. 4.4	Statements following a `case` label should be terminated by a statement that exits the `switch` statement.
Rec. 4.5	All `switch` statements should have a `default` clause.
Rule 4.6	Use `break` and `continue` instead of `goto`.
Rec. 4.7	Do not have overly complex functions.

See Also

Rec. 10.3: When to use selection statements.

Rec. 15.15: `for` loop variables.

Rule 4.1 Do not change
a loop variable inside a
`for` loop block.

Iteration statements are common in C++. The standard library provides a large number of algorithms that iterate through collections of objects. If you use the standard library you will be able to avoid many mistakes related to iteration, but we still consider it important to know how to write `for`, `do-while`, and `while` statements correctly.

When you write a `for` loop, it is highly confusing and error-prone to change the loop variable within the loop body rather than inside the expression executed after each iteration.

In order to be sure that the loop terminates, you need to know how the loop index is updated after each iteration and under which conditions the loop terminates. Perhaps the best feature of the `for` loop is that if it is used correctly, you can know the number of iterations by studying the `for` loop header. In general, avoid loop indexes that are modified in more than one place. Modify loop indexes only once, either before or after each iteration.

Rec. 4.2 Update loop
variables close to where
the loop condition is
specified.

It is important to consistently use the same method to solve the same problem. Your code will be hard to understand if you use `do-while`, `while`, and `for` loops in many different ways. It is better to have a preferred way for selecting an iteration statement. We recommend these guidelines:

- Use a `for` loop if the loop variable is updated on exit from the block *after* the loop condition has been checked.
- Use a `do-while` loop if the loop will execute at least once and if the loop variable is updated *before* the condition is checked.
- Use a `while` loop if the loop variable is updated on entry to the block *after* the loop condition has been checked.

These guidelines are easy to follow if you always choose the type of loop that allows you to update the loop variables as close as possible to where the loop condition is specified.

Rec. 4.3 All flow control
primitives (`if`, `else`,
`while`, `for`, `do`,
`switch`, and `case`)
should be followed by a
block, even if it is
empty.

Another way to make code much more reliable and easy to read is to enclose all code after flow control primitives in a block, even if it is empty.

EXAMPLE 4.1 **Block after a** `for` **loop**

```
const int numberOfObjects = 42;
EmcArray<EmcString> a(numberOfObjects);

for (int i = 0; i < numberOfObjects; i++)
{  // Recommended

   char buf[3];
   ostrstream os(buf, sizeof buf);
   os << i << ends;
   a[i] = buf;
}
```

EXAMPLE 4.2 **Blocks in a** `switch` **statement**

```
cout << "Enter value: ";
int value;
cin >> value;

switch (value)      // OK with block
{
   case 1:          // OK
   case 2:          // OK
   {
      cout << "1 or 2: " << a[value] << endl;
      break;
   }
   default:
   {
      if (value > 2 && value < numberOfObjects)
      {
         cout << "Not 1 or 2: " << a[value] << endl;
      }
      break;
   }
}
```

Note that it is OK to group several case labels after each other if the statements in the grouped cases do the same thing.

Rec. 4.4 Statements following a `case` label should be terminated by a statement that exits the `switch` statement.

Statements following a `case` label should be terminated by a statement that exits the switch statement, such as `return` or `break`. Leaving out such termination results in a fall-through between different cases, which in many cases is a bug. In some rare situations, fall-through is intentional, but this should be clearly documented in the code.

EXAMPLE 4.3   **How to write** `switch` **statements**

```
enum Status
{
   red,
   green
};


EmcString convertStatus(Status status)
{
   switch (status)
   {
      case red:
      {
         return EmcString("Red");    // OK, exits switch
      }
      case green:
      {
         return EmcString("Green");  // OK, exits switch
      }
      default:
      {
         return EmcString("Illegal value");
      }
   }
}
```

Rec. 4.5 All `switch` statements should have a `default` clause.

We recommend that all `switch` statements have a `default` clause. In some cases the default clause can never be reached because there are `case` labels for all possible enum values in the `switch` statement, but by having such an unreachable `default` clause you show a potential reader that you know what you are doing. By having such a `default` clause, you also provide for future changes. If an additional enum value is added, the `switch` statement should not just silently ignore the new value. Instead, it should in some way notify the programmer that the `switch` statement must be changed. For example, you could throw an exception or terminate the program.

Rule 4.6 Use break and continue instead of goto.
We are also banning the use of goto. Yes, there might be cases where the use of goto might make a program easier to maintain or understand, but in most cases this is unlikely.

Rethink your design and do your best to avoid goto. In most cases you can rewrite the code using break or continue. If you avoid goto, your code will be less sensitive to changes because it is illegal to jump with goto past an initialization of a variable.

EXAMPLE 4.4   **How to break out of a loop**

```
const int max = 10;
bool errorflag = false;

for(int i = 0; i < max; i++)
{
   // ...
   if (someCondition())
   {
      errorflag = true;
      break; // leaves loop
   }
}
// no goto needed
if (errorflag)
{
   abort();
}
```

Rec. 4.7 Do not have overly complex functions.
Anyone who has had to take over code written by someone else knows that complex code is hard to maintain. There are many ways in which a function can be complex, such as the number of lines of code, the number of parameters, or the number of possible paths through a function. The number of possible paths through a function, which depends on the number of control flow primitives, is the main source of function complexity. Therefore you should be aware that heavy use of control flow primitives will make your code more difficult to maintain.

chapter five

Object Life Cycle

There are a few things you should think about when declaring, initializing, and copying objects.

- You should have as few variables as possible in order to improve performance. This also means that you should not create a copy of an object unless you have to.
- You should not have to browse through many pages of code to find the declaration of a variable.
- You should not have to modify many pages of code if you want to change the value of a literal.
- Copying and initialization should always create objects with valid states.

Initialization of Variables and Constants

A little discipline when declaring and initializing variables and constants can do wonders to make your code easier to understand and maintain. What may come as a surprise is that you can also improve the performance of your program.

Rec. 5.1   Declare and initialize variables close to where they
are used.

Rec. 5.2   If possible, initialize variables at the point of declaration.

Rec. 5.3   Declare each variable in a separate declaration
statement.

Rec. 5.4   Literals should be used only in the definition of
constants and enumerations.

See Also   Rec. 1.2, Style A.4: Variable names.

Rule 7.10: How to access string literals.

**Rec. 5.1 Declare and
initialize variables close
to where they are used.**

It is best to declare variables close to where they are used. Otherwise you may have trouble finding out the type of a particular
variable. Another advantage of localized variable declarations is
more efficient code because only the objects that are actually
needed will be initialized.

EXAMPLE 5.1   **Initializing variables**

Instead of declaring the variable at the beginning of a code block
and giving it a value much later:

```
int i;

// 20 lines of code not using i

i = 10;          // No
```

try to declare and initialize the variable close to its first use:

```
int j = 10;      // Better
```

**Rec. 5.2 If possible,
initialize variables at the
point of declaration.**

Try to initialize a variable to a well-defined value at the point of
declaration. The main reason is to avoid redundant member function calls. Suppose you have a class with both a constructor and
an assignment operator taking the same type of argument. If you
assign an object of that class instead of using the corresponding
constructor, then two member function calls are needed to give
the object a proper value. The first call is to a default constructor

that must be provided when an object is declared without an initializer.

EXAMPLE 5.2   **Initialization instead of assignment**

```
// Not recommended
EmcString string1;            // calls default constructor
string1 = "hello";            // calls assignment operator

// Better
EmcString string2("hello"); // calls constructor
```

Initialization at the point of declaration can also remove many potential bugs from your code by reducing the risk of using an uninitialized object.

Variables of built-in types are a special case because they have no default constructors to be called when an initializer is missing. Instead, such variables remain uninitialized until they are assigned to, so if you do not initialize them, you should assign to them as soon as possible.

The reason such variables are not always initialized is that it is sometimes very difficult or even impossible to do so. Suppose, for example, that the variable must be passed to a function as a reference argument to be initialized.

EXAMPLE 5.3   **Assignment instead of initialization**

```
int i;       // no reason to initialize i
cin >> i;    // modifies both cin and i
```

Rec. 5.3 Declare each variable in a separate declaration statement.

Declaring multiple variables on the same line is not recommended. The code will be difficult to read and understand.

Separate declarations also make the code more readable and easier to comment, if you want to attach a comment to each variable.

Some common mistakes are also avoided. Remember that when you declare a pointer, a unary pointer is bound only to the variable that immediately follows.

EXAMPLE 5.4   **Declaring multiple variables**

```
int i, *ip, ia[100], (*ifp)();     // Not recommended

LoadModule* oldLm = 0;      // pointer to the old object
LoadModule* newLm = 0;      // pointer to the new object

// declares one int*, m, and one int, n.
int* m, n;                  // Not recommended
```

Rec. 5.4 Literals should be used only in the definition of constants and enumerations.

Literals should be used only in the definition of constants and enumerations.

One reason is that literals need an additional comment to be understood. Some integers such as 0 and 1 are exceptions because their meaning can often be deduced from the context in which they are used. Many of them can now be replaced by the new `bool` values, `true` and `false`.

Code with literals is also more difficult to maintain because they may be sprinkled all over the code.

EXAMPLE 5.5   **Correct use of literals**

```
// Literal in definition of const,
const size_t charMapSize = 256;

// but not to specify array size!
char charMap[charMapSize];

// Or for comparison!
for (int i = 0; i < charMapSize; i++)
{
    // ...
}
```

Constructor Initializer Lists

Base classes and nonstatic data members should be initialized in the constructor initializer list because this is more efficient than using assignment inside the body of the constructor.

RULES AND   Rec. 5.5   Initialize all data members.
RECOMMENDATIONS   Rule 5.6   Let the order in the initializer list be the same as
                                       the order of declaration in the header file: first base
                                       classes, then data members.
                       Rec. 5.7   Do not use or pass `this` in constructor initializer
                                       lists.

See Also   Rec. 1.2, Style A.5: Names of data members.
                       Rule 10.1: Access to data members.

Rec. 5.5 Initialize all   Initialization is the recommended way to give data members and
data members.   base classes proper values. All direct base classes, nonstatic data
                           members, and virtual base classes can have initializers in the con-
                           structor initializer list. If the object to be initialized is a class with
                           constructors, the expression determines what constructor to use.
                           If not, the expression could be a value to copy.

                           If you do not specify an initializer, the default constructor will be
                           used to initialize the data member or the base class, if such a con-
                           structor exists. Data members of a built-in type will not be initial-
                           ized, which can be very dangerous. Clearly this is not desirable.
                           Initializing integers to zero can sometimes be a good idea.

                           It is possible to give data members values inside the body instead
                           of in the initializer list. We do not recommend this practice
                           because it is less efficient to call first the default constructor and
                           then the assignment operator than to call only one constructor.
                           For data members of built-in types there is no such difference, but
                           for the sake of consistency, even these should be initialized in the
                           constructor initializer list.

                           There are some exceptions. If a data member must be initialized
                           by an expression that must access the containing object, it is
                           sometimes necessary to defer initialization to the body of the con-
                           structor. Another situation is when an expression is too complex
                           to appear in the initializer list.

                           Base classes are treated as data members in the initializer list,
                           which means that they are also initialized by the default construc-
                           tor if no initializer is provided.

EXAMPLE 5.6 **Constructor initializer lists**

```
class Base
{
   public:
      explicit Base(int i);
      Base();
   private:
      int iM;
};

Base::Base(int i) : iM(i) // iM must be initialized
{
   // Empty
}

Base::Base() : iM(0)      // iM must be initialized
{
   // Empty
}

class Derived : public Base
{
   public:
      explicit Derived(int i);
      Derived();
   private:
      int  jM;
      Base bM;
};

Derived::Derived(int i) // jM must be initialized
: Base(i), jM(i)        // Default constructor used for bM
{
   // Empty
}

Derived::Derived()    // jM must be initialized
: jM(0), bM(1)        // Default constructor used for Base
{
   // Empty
}
```

Rule 5.6 Let the order in the initializer list be the same as the order of declaration in the header file: first base classes, then data members.

It is legal C++ to list initializers in any order you wish, but you should list them in the same order as they will be called.

The order in the initializer list is irrelevant to the execution order of the initializers. Putting initializers for data members and base classes in any order other than their actual initialization order is therefore highly confusing and can lead to errors. A data member could be accessed before it is initialized if the order in the initializer list is incorrect.

Virtual base classes are always initialized first, then base classes, data members, and finally the constructor body for the most derived class is run.

EXAMPLE 5.7   **Order of initializers**

```
class Derived : public Base     // Base is number 1
{
    public:
        explicit Derived(int i);
        Derived();
    private:
        int   jM;                 // jM is number 2
        Base bM;                  // bM is number 3
};

Derived::Derived(int i) : Base(i), jM(i), bM(i)
// Recommended order          1        2      3
{
    // Empty
}
```

Rec. 5.7 Do not use or pass this in constructor initializer lists.

Another unsafe practice is to use or pass this in the initializer list. The object pointed at by this is not fully constructed until the body of the constructor is run.

The object is not fully constructed when base classes and data members are initialized. Calling a virtual member function through a pointer or reference to the partially constructed object makes your program likely to crash.

Calling a member function in a member initializer list can be equally dangerous, since such a member function could try to access uninitialized members of the class. Passing this to base class and member initializers, or using `this` implicitly by calling a member function in the initializer list, should therefore be avoided as much as possible.

Copying of Objects

As a rule, you should avoid copying as much as possible, but it is sometimes necessary to copy objects and you need to know when. It is equally important to understand when copying is inappropriate.

Copying can be done by initialization or by assignment. Copying by assignment is similar to initialization but is more difficult because you modify an existing object that may hold resources that must be correctly managed.

The compiler will generate a copy constructor and a copy assignment operator if the class does not declare one. It is important to understand when the compiler-generated ones are appropriate.

RULES AND RECOMMENDATIONS	Rec. 5.8	**Avoid unnecessary copying of objects that are costly to copy.**
	Rule 5.9	**A function must never return, or in any other way give access to, references or pointers to local variables outside the scope in which they are declared.**
	Rec. 5.10	**If objects of a class should never be copied, then the copy constructor and the copy assignment operator should be declared** `private` **and not implemented.**
	Rec. 5.11	**A class that manages resources should declare a copy constructor, a copy assignment operator, and a destructor.**
	Rule 5.12	**Copy assignment operators should be protected from doing destructive actions if an object is assigned to itself.**

See Also   Rec. 7.3–Rec. 7.5, Rule 7.6: Argument passing.

Rule 7.7: Return value of copy assignment operator.

Rule 5.9: Parameter type for copy constructor and copy assignment operator.

Rec. 12.7, Rule 12.8: Resource management.

Rec. 5.8 Avoid
unnecessary copying of
objects that are costly to
copy.

Copying an object is not the same as making a bitwise copy of its storage. Bitwise copying, for example through the use of `memcpy()`, works only for a limited number of objects and should almost always be avoided.

For most objects, copying is the same as calling the copy constructor or the assignment operator for the class. Because a class could have other objects as data members or inherit from other classes, many member function calls would be needed to copy the object. To improve performance, you should not copy an object unless it is necessary.

It is possible to avoid copying by using pointers and references to objects, but then you will instead have to worry about the lifetime of objects. You must understand when it is necessary to copy an object and when it is not.

Rule 5.9 A function
must never return, or in
any other way give
access to, references or
pointers to local
variables outside the
scope in which they are
declared.

Returning a pointer or reference to a local variable is always wrong because it gives the user a pointer or reference to an object that no longer exists. Such a pointer or reference cannot be used without the risk of overwriting the caller's stack space. Most compilers warn about this, but it is still possible to make mistakes.

EXAMPLE 5.8   **Returning dangling pointers and references**

```
int& dangerous()
{
   int i = 5;
   return i;              // NO: Reference to local returned
}

int& j = dangerous(); // NO: j is dangerous to use

// much later:

cout << j;               // Crash, boom, bang, program dies
```

There are less obvious ways of making the same mistake, as in this example:

```
struct MyStruct
{
   char *p;
   // ...
};

MyStruct ms;

void alsoDangerous()
{
   const char str[] = "Bad news up ahead";
   ms.p = str;          // No: address of local stored
}

alsoDangerous();

cout << ms.p << endl; // Garbage printed
```

The function `alsoDangerous()` does not explicitly pass any
pointer or reference to any local object, but it lets such a pointer
leak through by assigning it to a struct with a scope larger than
the local data in the function. The result in this case is that gar-
bage is printed when operator `<<()` tries to access an object that
no longer exists.

Rec. 5.10 If objects of a
class should never be
copied, then the copy
constructor and the
copy assignment
operator should be
declared `private` and
not implemented.

Before you implement copy constructors and copy assignment
operators for a class, you should ask yourself whether the class
has a reasonable copy semantics. Is it reasonable to be able to
copy an object of the class? Sometimes this is a very simple question to answer, such as for a string class, which of course should
be copyable. In many other cases the question about copying can
be quite hard to answer. But remember that even if you cannot
copy objects, you can still copy pointers, and that is often sufficient.

Ideally the question of copy semantics for a class will naturally
come out of the design process. Do not push copy semantics on a
class that should not have it.

By declaring the copy constructor and copy assignment operator
as `private`, you can make a class noncopyable. These member
functions must be declared because the compiler would otherwise
generate a public copy constructor and a public copy assignment
operator for the class. The two privately declared member func-

tions should not be called, which means they do not have to be implemented, only declared.

EXAMPLE 5.9   **Noncopyable class**

```
class CommunicationPort
{
    public:
        explicit CommunicationPort(int port);
        ~CommunicationPort();
        // ...
    private:
        CommunicationPort(const CommunicationPort& cp);
        CommunicationPort&
            operator=(const CommunicationPort& cp);
        // ...
};
```

Rec. 5.11 A class that manages resources should declare a copy constructor, a copy assignment operator, and a destructor.

As said before, the compiler will generate a copy constructor, a copy assignment operator, and a destructor if these member functions have not been declared. A compiler-generated copy constructor does memberwise initialization and a compiler-generated copy assignment operator does memberwise assignment of data members and base classes. For some classes, the generated member functions have the wrong behavior and must be implemented. Classes that manage resources belong to this category. We have to make sure that a resource is acquired and released only once.

EXAMPLE 5.10   **String class without copy constructor**

A string class usually has to provide a copy constructor, an assignment operator, and a destructor, because it stores a pointer to memory allocated with new.

```
class DangerousString
{
    public:
        DangerousString();
        DangerousString(const char* cp);
        // No: must provide copy constructor,
        // copy assignment operator!
```

```
        ~DangerousString();
        // ...

    private:
        char* cpM;
};

DangerousString::DangerousString(const char* cp)
: cpM(new char[strlen(cp)+1])
{
    strcpy(cpM, cp);
}

DangerousString::~DangerousString()
{
    delete [] cpM;
}
```

The generated copy constructor and copy assignment operator will copy the pointer, not the character array. Two objects will store a pointer to the same character array after a call to one of these member functions. If we implement a destructor that deletes the pointer, but we do not provide a copy constructor, the pointer will be dangling when the first object's destructor is called.

```
DangerousString s1;

{
    DangerousString s2("test");
    s1 = s2;
    // ...
}
// Dangerous to access s1 here
```

EXAMPLE 5.11   Copyable class that manages memory

EmcIntStack is a simple stack class that manages an array of integers. Because we want to be able to copy stack objects, we declare the copy constructor, the assignment operator, and the destructor as public members of the class.

```
// EmcIntStack is copyable

class EmcIntStack
{
    public:
        EmcIntStack();
        EmcIntStack(const EmcIntStack& s);
        ~EmcIntStack();
        EmcIntStack& operator=(const EmcIntStack& s);
        // ...
    private:
        enum     { defaultSizeM = 100 };
        unsigned  allocatedM;
        int*      vectorM;
        int       topM;
};

EmcIntStack::EmcIntStack()
: allocatedM(defaultSizeM),
  vectorM(new int[allocatedM]),
  topM(0)
{
}

EmcIntStack::EmcIntStack(const EmcIntStack& s)
: allocatedM(s.allocatedM),
  vectorM(new int[allocatedM]),
  topM(s.topM)
{
}

EmcIntStack::~EmcIntStack()
{
    delete [] vectorM;
}
```

We will study the assignment operator when explaining the next rule.

Rule 5.12 Copy assignment operators should be protected from doing destructive actions if an object is assigned to itself.

When implementing the copy assignment operator we must make sure that self-assignment does not corrupt the state of the object. There is a risk that you might delete pointers and then assign them to themselves. To prevent that, you could copy the new state of the object to local variables before assigning to the data members. This always works, but is less efficient than assigning to the data members directly. The most common solution is to check the address of the object passed as an argument before modifying the state of the object. If the current object is passed as argument, the copy assignment operator simply returns without modifying the object.

EXAMPLE 5.12   **Self-assignment**

```
EmcString s = "Aguirre";
s = s;                          // Self assignment
cout << s << endl;              // Should print "Aguirre"
```

EXAMPLE 5.13   **Implementing a copy assignment operator**

When implementing the copy assignment operator for the EmcIntStack described above, we check the this-pointer before modifying the object. This is necessary because we want to be able to reuse already allocated memory instead of allocating new memory after each assignment.

```
EmcIntStack& EmcIntStack::operator=(const EmcIntStack& s)
{
   if (this != &s)
   {
      int* newVector = vectorM;
      if (allocatedM <= s.topM)
      {
         // operator new may throw bad_alloc
         newVector = new int[s.allocatedM];
      }
      // copy elements
      memcpy(newVector, s.vectorM, s.topM * sizeof(int));

      if (vectorM != newVector)
      {
         // release memory
         delete [] vectorM;
         vectorM = newVector;
      }

      // assign to object

      allocatedM = s.allocatedM;
      topM       = s.topM;
   }
   return *this;
}
```

Another similar class is our string class, `EmcString`. As in most other string classes, objects of this class have a character array to store the value of the string. `EmcString` has two data members, `cpM` and `lengthM`. When assigning to a string, we simply deallocate the character array pointed at by `cpM` and create a new one of appropriate size before copying the string.

```
class EmcString
{
   public:
      // ...
      EmcString& operator=(const EmcString& s);
      size_t length() const;
      // ...
   private:
      size_t lengthM;
      char*  cpM;
};
```

Instead of checking the `this`-pointer, we make sure that self-assignment does not corrupt the state of the object by making a copy of the argument before modifying the string. This will be slightly more efficient except when the parameter string is the same object as the one assigned to. This could be considered a special case that is not worth optimizing for. An even more efficient solution would be to avoid memory allocation altogether when the existing string is big enough, as in the previous example.

```
EmcString& EmcString::operator=(const EmcString& s)
{
   // Not optimized for self-assignment
   char* tmp = new char[s.length() + 1];
   strcpy(tmp, s.cpM);
   delete [] cpM;
   cpM  = tmp;
   lengthM = s.lengthM;

   return *this;
}
```

chapter six

Conversions

It can be difficult to understand C++ code that uses implicit type conversions between otherwise unrelated types. A number of techniques can be used to prevent such problems. Some conversions are so dangerous that most compilers will give you a warning. We will show you how to avoid the dangers involved by providing a few guidelines.

RULES AND RECOMMENDATIONS	Rec. 6.1	Use explicit rather than implicit type conversions.
	Rec. 6.2	Use the new cast operators (`dynamic_cast`, `const_cast`, `reinterpret_cast`, and `static_cast`) instead of the old-style casts, unless portability is an issue.
	Rec. 6.3	Do not cast away `const`.
	Rule 6.4	Declare a data member `mutable` if it must be modified by a `const` member function.

See Also Rec. 7.18–Rec. 7.19: Conversion functions.

Rec. 6.1 Use explicit rather than implicit type conversions.

Most conversions are bad in some way. They can make the code less portable, less robust, and less readable. It is therefore important to use only explicit conversions. Implicit conversions are almost always bad.

It is common to use different integral types in a program. It can be dangerous to mix different types because the size and layout of these types vary. A value that may fit in a `short` on one platform is truncated on another platform, for example. By always having explicit conversions, it is much easier to find potentially dangerous code.

It is also common for a class to provide an implicit conversion to its representation. This makes it possible to pass an object as argument to functions expecting direct access to the representation. If such conversions are needed, we do not recommend using a conversion operator function to do the job. You should instead have a member function that does the conversion for you.

EXAMPLE 6.1   Explicit conversions

```
const unsigned large = 456789;

// Potentially dangerous conversion
const int     size  = (int)large;
```

EXAMPLE 6.2   Conversion of a string object to `const char*`

It is common that a string class provides an implicit conversion to a `const char*`. This makes it possible to pass a string object as argument to functions expecting such a pointer.

```
class DangerousString
{
    public:
        // ...
        DangerousString(const char* cp);
        // ...
        operator const char*() const;    // Not recommended
        const char* cStr() const;        // Recommended
        // ...
};
```

If your string class provides both a conversion operator member function and an ordinary member function, you should always use the latter. If only a conversion operator function is provided, you should use only explicit conversions.

```
EmcStack<const char*> stack;
stack.push("one");

DangerousString two("two");

// Not recommended to store the result of a conversion.
// Implicit conversion is not recommended.
stack.push(two);                    // Implicit conversion

DangerousString three("three");
// Explicit conversion is better than
// implicit conversion.
stack.push((const char*)three); // Explicit conversion

DangerousString four("four");
// Member function call is better than
// conversion operator function call.
stack.push(four.cStr());          // Member function call
```

Rec. 6.2 Use the new cast operators (`dynamic_cast`, `const_cast`, `reinterpret_cast`, and `static_cast`) instead of the old-style casts, unless portability is an issue.

There are many ways to convert values in C++: the traditional C cast notation, the functional notation, and new-style casts. The first two are explained in most introductory C++ books. A new-style cast means that one of the four new cast operators:

- `static_cast`
- `reinterpret_cast`
- `dynamic_cast`
- `const_cast`

is being used. If your compiler supports the new cast operators you should use them instead of the traditional cast operators because they give the user a way to distinguish between different types of casts.

A good thing about these operators is that their behavior is well-defined in situations where the behavior of an ordinary cast is undefined, or at least ambiguous. They cannot remove all dangers involved in type conversions, but they are far better than the traditional cast syntax. In order to use them, you must understand when each one of them is appropriate.

A static cast is similar to an ordinary cast except that it does not allow you to cast away constness or cast between unrelated types. You can replace all implicit conversions with `static_cast` expressions.

Whenever you can make an implicit conversion from one type to another, you can make a `static_cast` in the opposite direction. For example, you can use static casts for base-to-derived conversions if the base class is nonvirtual.

The operator `const_cast` is solely used for casting away `const`.

The operator `reinterpret_cast` is used when casting between unrelated types (for example, when casting an `int*` to a `char*`).

The operator `dynamic_cast` checks the type of its operand at run-time. It is similar to a `static_cast`, but it is safer. It can be used only for types with run time-type information, that is, classes with at least one virtual member function, also called polymorphic classes. It also allows base-to-derived conversions when the base class is virtual. Because there is a run time penalty for using `dynamic_cast` instead of `static_cast`, you should use it only when it is absolutely necessary.

A problem with these operators is that they are not yet supported by all compilers. Therefore, if you anticipate porting your code to another environment, you should consider avoiding them for portability reasons.

EXAMPLE 6.3   **Using** `static_cast`

```
const unsigned large = 456789;
const int      size  = static_cast<const int>(large);

EmcStack<const char*> stack;
EmcString three("three");

// Not recommended to store the result of a conversion.
// static_cast is better than old-style cast.
stack.push(static_cast<const char*>(three));
```

EXAMPLE 6.4   **New style casts**

```
class B
{
   public:
      // ...
      virtual ~B();
};
```

```
class D : virtual public B
{
   public:
      // ...
      virtual ~D();
};

class E
{
   public:
      // ...
      virtual ~E();
};

D* dynamicCast(B* b)
{
   // Must use dynamic_cast when base class is virtual.
   return dynamic_cast<D*>(b);
}

D* constCast(const D* d1)
{
   // Should use const_cast when casting away const.
   return const_cast<D*>(d1);
}

E* reinterpretCast(D* d)
{
   // Should use reinterpret_cast when casting pointer
   // to pointer of unrelated type.
   return reinterpret_cast<E*>(d);
}
```

Rec. 6.3 Do not cast away const.

Generally, you should not cast away the constness of objects. However, there are a few rare cases where casting away constness is permitted, such as if you need to use a function that has incorrectly specified a parameter as non-const even if it does not modify it. If you have been passed a const object and need to pass it to a function that takes a non-const object as parameter, then you are forced to choose between two evils. You could modify your own function so that you will be passed a non-const object. This is not fair because it will only pass the problem to your user. Instead, you should solve the problem by maintaining your const-correct interface and cast away the constness of the object before you pass it to the function you need to use.

There are other problems with casting away const, such as the fact that const objects might reside in write-protected memory. If you change such an object, the runtime system will probably report an error.

EXAMPLE 6.5   Casting away const

```
// NOT RECOMMENDED
// Parameter should be of type const EmcString&
void addToFileList(EmcString& s); // does not modify s

void addFiles(const EmcArray<EmcString>& s)
{
   size_t max = s.size();
   for(size_t i = 0; i < max; i++)
   {
      // casting away const is NOT RECOMMENDED
      // s[i] returns const EmcString&
      addToFileList((EmcString&) s[i]);
      // ...
   }
}
```

EXAMPLE 6.6   Object in write-protected memory

```
// ci may be in write-protected memory
const int ci = 22;

int* pi = (int*) &ci; // NO: Const cast away

// reading write-protected memory?
int i = *pi;          // OK

// writing into write-protected memory?
*pi = 7;              // NO: This MAY fail!!!
```

Rule 6.4 Declare a data member mutable if it must be modified by a const member function.

If an object caches computed values for the sake of efficiency, such data members should be declared mutable because that makes them modifiable inside const member functions.

EXAMPLE 6.7   **Class with a** `mutable` **data member**

```
class EmcMatrix
{
   public:
      double determinant() const;
      // ...
   private:
      mutable bool   isDirtyM;          // mutable
      mutable double detM;              // mutable
      double calculateDeterminant() const;
      // ...
};

double EmcMatrix::determinant() const
{
   if(isDirtyM)
   {
      // OK, access to mutable data members
      detM = calculateDeterminant();
      isDirtyM = false;
   }
   return detM;
}
```

The member function `determinant()` was declared `const` even though it changed data members of the class. This was made possible by declaring these data members `mutable`.

If your compiler does not support `mutable` data members, then the best solution is to cast away `const` inside the function and add a comment to show other readers of the code that you had no other option in order to keep the interface `const`-correct.

The Class Interface

The class interface is the most important part of a class. Sophisticated algorithms will not help if the class interface is wrong. Different aspects of the class interface are discussed in this chapter.

- Inline functions
- Argument passing
- `const`ness
- Operator and function overloading
- Conversion operator functions

Inline Functions

Inline functions can improve the performance of your program. This chapter discusses which functions should be specified as inline and which should not.

Rec. 7.1   **Make simple functions inline.**

Rule 7.2   **Do not declare virtual member functions** `inline`.

See Also   Rec. 14.1: The danger of having too many inline functions.

Rule 14.2: How to avoid making a virtual destructor inline.

Example 2.5: How to temporarily disable inlining.

Rec. 7.1 Make simple
functions inline.

It is possible to improve performance and make programs smaller by declaring functions inline. By the same token, using inlining in the wrong places makes programs larger and less efficient.

Fewer machine instructions are executed when an inline function is called because there is no need to prepare a stack frame for the function call. As long as the program does not grow so that the code resides on different pages in memory, this is likely to improve performance. Too-large executables should be avoided, so it is difficult to give an exact advice on when to use inline functions.

It may come as a surprise that inline expansion could decrease the overall size of the program, but if the overhead of a function call is larger than the total size of the inline-expanded code, this is actually true.

If you have member functions whose sole purpose is to give access to data members, those member functions are likely candidates for inlining. This is because a class should not have any public or protected data members. Because member functions should be used instead, you should probably make them inline for the reasons explained above.

It can be hard to know exactly when inlining is appropriate, so our advice is to be cautious. Consider inlining only when you know that the code generated for the function is small.

EXAMPLE 7.1 **A class with inline member functions**

```
class Point
{
   public:
      Point(double x, double y);
      // ...
      // accessors
      double x() const;
      double y() const;

      // modifiers
      void   x(double x);
      void   y(double y);

   private:
      double xM;
      double yM;
};

inline
double Point::x() const
{
   return xM;
}

// ...

Point operator+(const Point& p1, const Point& p2)
{
   return Point(p1.x() + p2.x(), p1.y() + p2.y());
}
```

A drawback of making a member function inline is that all client code must be recompiled each time the member function changes. This is especially annoying in larger projects with many unstable classes that are used in many places. If this is your situation, consider having all member functions non-inline. By using inline definition files, you can do that without much effort.

Rule 7.2 Do not declare virtual member functions inline.

Virtual member functions could often be simple enough for inlining, but unfortunately they should not be declared inline. If a class with virtual member functions is used, some compilers will require that all virtual member functions have implementations that are linked with the program. The reason is that the address of a virtual member function is needed when a function call is dynamically bound. Most compilers generate a table with the address of all virtual member functions, also called the virtual table.

Because inline functions are inline-expanded, they do not have an implementation by default. However, if we make an inline function virtual, it must have a definition. Such a definition will then be generated by the compiler; because the inline function is defined in a header file, there is no obvious place to put it. A good place could be in the same object file that contains the definition of the virtual table for the class. What makes things complicated is the fact that the compiler does not always have an obvious place for the virtual table either.

The virtual table must be allocated in one of the object modules. Some compilers allocate it in the object module that contains the definition of the first virtual function of the class. If the first virtual function is inline, the virtual table as well as code for all virtual member functions that are inline could be generated in each object module that uses the class.

All this may seem complicated and it is. This may not be a problem in the future, but with the compilers of today you should avoid having virtual functions that are inline.

Argument Passing and Return Values

Calling member functions is the normal way to make things happen in a C++ program, but ordinary functions are also used. Your code will be easier to understand if function parameters and return values are declared in a consistent way. You can also improve the performance of your code.

RULES AND RECOMMENDATIONS

Rec. 7.3	**Pass arguments of built-in types by value unless the function should modify them.**	
Rec. 7.4	**Use a parameter of pointer type only if the function stores the address or passes it to a function that does.**	
Rec. 7.5	**Pass arguments of class types by reference or pointer.**	
Rule 7.6	**Pass arguments of class types by reference or pointer if the class is meant as a public base class.**	

> **Rule 7.7** The copy assignment operator should return a non-`const` reference to the object assigned to.

See Also Rule 5.12: How to implement copy assignment operator.

Rule 7.8 – Rule 7.9: Constness of pointer or reference argument.

Rec. 10.2: Validity of pointers and references returned from member functions.

Rec. 15.9: Passing integers.

Rec. 7.3 Pass arguments of built-in types by value unless the function should modify them.

Arguments to functions can be passed in three ways: by value, by pointer, and by reference.

EXAMPLE 7.2 **Different types of function parameters**

```
void    valueFunc(T  t);      // By value
void   pointerFunc(T* tp);    // By pointer
void referenceFunc(T& tr);    // By reference
```

Passing arguments by value means that the function parameters are copies of the arguments. If the parameters are pointers or references, the function has access to the arguments. But remember that if an argument is a temporary created by an implicit type cast, the object used to create that temporary will not by modified.

A good practice is to pass built-in types such as `char`, `int`, and `double` by value because it is cheap to copy such variables. This recommendation is also valid for some objects of classes that are cheap to copy, such as simple aggregates of a very small number of built-in types, such as a class that represents complex numbers that often just consists of two `double`s as data members.

If a function needs access to an argument, then you must pass also built-in types by reference or pointer. This should otherwise be avoided.

EXAMPLE 7.3 **Passing parameters by value**

```
void func(char c);              // OK
void func(int i);               // OK
void func(double d);            // OK
void func(complex<float> c);    // OK
```

Rec. 7.4 Use a parameter of pointer type only if the function stores the address or passes it to a function that does.

Reference and pointer parameters are similar in that both allow a function to modify the arguments. We recommend pointer parameters only if a function stores the pointer value or if it passes it to another function that does.

Some programmers argue that the code is easier to understand if pointer arguments are used when the function modifies an object, because then you must take the addresses of objects when such functions are called. This would make it obvious, from reading the client code, when a function modifies an argument.

Unfortunately, the implementation of a function is often more difficult to read if pointer parameters are dereferenced inside expressions. Local references make it easier to understand such complicated expressions. The problem with this solution is that one more local variable is needed. This makes the function slightly more complex.

Pointer parameters also force the implementation to consider how null pointers are handled because dereferencing a null pointer is a fatal error that certainly will crash your program. References cannot be null, which relieves the implementation of the problem of checking whether it is null.

The implementation of a function taking a pointer as parameter might pass it to some other function, which in turn might also be passed a null pointer. It is easy to see that all this easily cascades to endless tests of pointer values.

Therefore, we recommend pointers only as a way of showing to the user that the address of the argument is stored by the function for later use, or is passed to a function that does so. Functions with pointer parameters must therefore be treated specially because the client must not delete objects whose addresses are passed to such a function. You should be suspicious if the address of a local object is passed to a function. One benefit of avoiding pointer parameters is that dangling pointers to local objects are easier to detect.

Unless you are careful, you may end up using pointer parameters everywhere in a system, reasoning that "I use a pointer in my interface because internally I have to call that other interface, which takes a pointer as argument." Thus, the use of pointer parameters can easily spread over a complete program system.

EXAMPLE 7.4 **Pointer and reference arguments**

EmcMathVector represents a two-dimensional vector.

```
class EmcMathVector
{
   public:
      EmcMathVector(double x, double y);
      EmcMathVector& operator*=(double factor);

      double x() const;
      double y() const;
      void   x(double x);
      void   y(double y);
      // ...
   private:
      double xM;
      double yM;
};

EmcMathVector::EmcMathVector(double x, double y)
: xM(x), yM(y)
{
   // empty
}

EmcMathVector& EmcMathVector::operator*=(double factor)
{
   xM *= factor;
   yM *= factor;

   return *this;
}
```

The question is how we implement a function that modifies the state of an EmcMathVector object. We could pass either a pointer or reference.

```
EmcMathVector v(1.2, 3.4);

// Not recommended
magnify(&v, 4.0);          // passing pointer

// Recommended
magnify(v,  4.0);          // passing reference
```

By looking at the implementation, we can see that the implementation of the function taking a pointer is slightly more complex.

```
// Pointer argument

void magnify(EmcMathVector* v, double factor)
// Not recommended to pass pointer
{
   if (v)               // Pointers might be 0
   {
      *v *= factor;   // scalar multiplication of vector
   }
   // Handle null pointers here in some way:
   // assert or exception
}


// Reference argument

void magnify(EmcMathVector& v, double factor)
// Recommended to pass reference
{
   v *= factor;         // scalar multiplication of vector
}
```

Rec. 7.5 Pass arguments of class types by reference or pointer.

Arguments of class type are often costly to copy, so we recommend that you pass a reference (or in some cases a pointer), preferably declared const, to such objects. Const access guarantees that the function will not change the argument, and when you pass a reference, the argument is not copied.

```
void func(const EmcString& s);          // const reference
```

Small objects are sometimes more efficient to pass by value, but by default we assume that arguments of class types are passed as const references. It is a good idea to always read the documentation for the class to determine whether an object should be passed by value or by const reference.

Template parameters are a problem here, because when you declare template functions, in many cases you may not know whether a user will pass a built-in or a class type. The thing to do is to select a way of passing parameters by looking at how costly it will be to copy an object of a type that is a template parameter. If you anticipate cheap copying, then you should pass parameters by value. Otherwise, use references.

EXAMPLE 7.5   **Passing arguments of unknown type**

A simplified version of the `vector` class in the standard library is a good example of what assumptions about types that are template parameters can be made. `InputIterator` is an argument to a member template and is expected to behave as a pointer. Because pointers should be cheap to copy, `InputIterator` parameters are passed by value. `T` is the type of the object stored in the vector, and because the class should work even when `T` is expensive to copy, `T` parameters are passed as references. `T` pointers, on the other hand, are passed by value.

```
template <class T>
class vector
{
    public:
        template <class InputIterator>
          vector(InputIterator first, InputIterator last);
        T*   begin();
        T&   operator[](size_t n);
        void push_back(const T& x);
        T*   insert(T* position, const T& x = T());
        // ...
};
```

Note: Member templates are a recent addition to the language. They are motivated by the fact that it is impossible to create smart pointer templates that smoothly replace the ordinary pointers without this new language feature, but there are other uses for them as well. With member template constructors, it is possible to allow a template instantiation to provide a conversion from an otherwise unrelated type to itself. Remember that two template instantiations are different types.

You can instantiate `vector<T>::vector` with any type that behaves as an `InputIterator`. This means that it is up to the client to decide whether built-in arrays or iterator classes are used to initialize the `vector<T>` object. Without member templates, it would have been necessary to make a decision when designing the template.

Rule 7.6 Pass arguments of class types by reference or pointer if the class is meant as a public base class.

If a class is meant to be a public base class, then you should always pass such objects by pointer or reference. As previously described, this will almost always give you better performance, but there are other reasons as well. If a function takes a reference or a pointer to a base class, objects of derived classes can also be used as arguments because C++ allows a pointer of reference to a public base class to be bound to a derived class object. This is an example of polymorphism, or the ability to use the same piece of code for different types of objects.

Say you unintentionally declare a function to have a value parameter instead of a reference parameter. As a result, when you try to pass a derived class object to the function, you will operate upon a base class object that is a copy of the base class part of the object. The compiler will not complain, but the function will probably not do what you expect.

You can avoid that problem by having only abstract base classes, or by making the copy constructor private or protected. Because an object of an abstract base class cannot be copied and thus created, the compiler will catch errors of this kind.

EXAMPLE 7.6   **Passing a base class reference**

```
// basic_ostream<charT, traits> is a public base class

template <class charT, class traits = file_traits<charT> >
class basic_ofstream
    : public basic_ostream<charT, traits>
{
   public:
      explicit basic_ofstream(const char* s,
                              openmode mode = out | trunc);
      // ...
};

typedef basic_ostream<char> ostream;
typedef basic_ofstream<char> ofstream;

ostream& operator<<(ostream& o, const EmcMathVector& v)
{
   o << v.x() << ", " << v.y();
   return o;
}

ofstream out("hello.txt");
EmcMathVector v(1.2, 5.5);

out << v << endl;
// operator<<(ostream&, const EmcMathVector&) called
```

In this case an `ofstream` object is passed to the `operator<<`, taking a reference to its base class `ostream`.

EXAMPLE 7.7   **Passing a base class object by value**

It is not possible to pass an object of the class `ostream` by value, because an `ostream` object cannot be copied.

```
void uselessPrint(ostream o, const EmcMathVector& v)
// NO: Compile error
{
    o << v.x() << ", " << v.y();
}
```

Rule 7.7 The copy assignment operator should return a non-`const` reference to the object assigned to.

The return value from the copy assignment operator should always be a non-`const` reference to the object assigned to. There are many reasons for this. One is that this is the return value of a compiler-generated copy assignment operator. It could be confusing if hand-written copy assignment operators had a different signature than the compiler-generated ones. Another reason is that all classes with copy semantics in the standard library have copy assignment operators with non-`const` return values.

EXAMPLE 7.8   **Return value from assignment operators**

The following expression is legal when using an `int*` to access an int-array:

```
int*      array = new int(3);
int*      arrayPointer
*(arrayPointer = array) = 42
```

If we instead use a smart pointer class to access the array, we want to keep this behavior for objects of that class.

```
EmcAutoArrayPtr<int> smartArrayPointer;
*(smartArrayPointer = array) = 42;
```

This requires that the copy construtor returns a non-cont reference to an object of the class.

---

const **Correctness**

Being "const correct"—correctly declaring function parameters, return values, variables and member functions as const or not—is important when writing code in C++.

Rule 7.8   A pointer or reference parameter should be declared const if the function does not change the object bound to it.

Rule 7.9   The copy constructor and copy assignment operator should always have a const reference as a parameter.

Rule 7.10   Use only const char pointers to access string literals.

Rule 7.11   A member function that does not change the state of the program should be declared const.

Rule 7.12   A member function that gives non-const access to the representation of an object must not be declared const.

Rec. 7.13   Do not let const member functions change the state of the program.

See Also   Rule 5.12: How to implement copy assignment operator.

Rule 7.7: Return value of copy assignment operator.

Rule 7.8 A pointer or reference parameter should be declared const if the function does not change the object bound to it.

Functions often have const reference or const pointer parameters to indicate that an argument is not modified by the function. An advantage of const-declared parameters is that the compiler will actually give you an error if you modify such a parameter by mistake, thus helping you to avoid bugs in the implementation.

EXAMPLE 7.9 `const`-**declared parametersm**

```
// operator<< does not modify the EmcString parameter
ostream& operator<<(ostream& out, const EmcString& s);
```

When an argument is passed by value, it is used to initialize a function parameter that will be a copy of the argument. The caller is therefore immune to changes made to that parameter by the called function. If you declare the parameter as `const` in these circumstances you will just be preventing any change to the parameter taking place in the body of the function. This would be of little help because not being able to change a parameter passed by value only puts unnecessary constraints on the programmer implementing the function. If a parameter passed by value is declared `const`, the value must be copied to a local variable if the value is to be modified by the function.

By not declaring the parameter `const`, you can use the argument value without first copying the value.

EXAMPLE 7.10 **Using a parameter as a local variable**

```
template <class T>
T arraySum(const EmcArray<T>& array,
           size_t first,
           size_t last)
{
   assert(last <= array.length());

   T sum = 0;
   // It is possible to update first because
   // it has not been declared const.

   for( ;first < last; first++)
   {
      sum += array[first];
   }

   return sum;
}
```

Rule 7.9 The copy
constructor and copy
assignment operator
should always have a
const reference as a
parameter.

Two particularly important examples of const parameters are
the copy constructors and the copy assignment operators, which
should always have a const reference as a parameter. In almost
all cases it is evident that they should not change the object copied from. Also if they have non-const reference parameters, constant objects of the class cannot be copied.

If a class does not allow constant objects to be copied, it cannot
be used in many situations where the programmer expects these
properties to hold, for example, when the class is used as a template argument, base class, or data member.

There is also a risk that the non-const parameters propagate to
other users of the class.

If a class inherits another class and provides a copy constructor, the implementation should probably initialize the base
class object using the copy constructor of the base class with
the copied object as argument. If the base class copy constructor has a non-const reference parameter and the derived class
copy constructor has a const reference parameter, then we
must cast away constness of the parameter, which we want to
avoid.

The same problem arises when such a class is used as a data
member.

EXAMPLE 7.11   Copyable type parameter

The following template assumes that the type argument T is copyable.

```
// Interface

// T is Copyable
template<class T>
class EmcStack
{
    public:
        // ...
```

```
                    void push(const T& t);
                    // ...
                private:
                    size_t  allocatedM;
                    size_t  topM;
                    T*      repM;
        };


        // Implementation

        // EmcAutoArrayPtr manages arrays of objects

        template <class T>
        void EmcStack<T>::push(const T& t)
        {
            if (topM == allocatedM) // allocate more memory
            {
                size_t newSize = 2 * allocatedM;
                EmcAutoArrayPtr<T> newRep(new T[newSize]);

                for(size_t i = 0; i < topM; i++)
                {
                    newRep[i] = repM[i];
                }

                repM = newRep.release();
                allocatedM = newSize;
            }

            // Works only if T is of a type that allows copying
            // of constants.
            repM[topM] = t;
            topM++;
        }
```

Rule 7.10 Use only const char pointers to access string literals.

Constness is not always as enforced by the language. A very simple example is string literals that are non-const. It is best to always access such strings through const char pointers, so that they cannot be modified. What is not commonly known is that according to the language definition followed by most compilers today, they are of non-const type.

Note: The standardization committee for C++ recently changed this, so that string literals are now `const`. However, it will take some time before compilers implement this new behavior, so we have kept this rule for the time being.

When you use a `const char*` instead, the compiler will prevent you from modifying the string literal through the pointer.

Unfortunately, this does not guard you from direct assignment to the pointer itself. It is therefore better to either `const` declare the pointer or use array notation, because it is not possible to assign to a built-in array.

EXAMPLE 7.12 **Accessing string literals**

```
// NOT RECOMMENDED
char*           message1  = "Calling Orson";

// Better
const char*     message2  = "Ice Hockey";

// Even better
const char* const message3  = "Terminator";

// Best
const char      message4[] = "I like candy";
```

Rule 7.11 A member function that does not change the state of the program should be declared `const`.

You should declare all member functions that do not modify the state of the program as `const`. Declaring a member function as `const` has two important implications:

- Only `const` member functions can be called for `const` objects.
- A `const` member function will not change data members.

It is a common error to forget to `const` declare member functions that should be `const`. If you forget to do this, it will be difficult to pass const references or pointers to objects of that class as arguments to functions. It will also be difficult to use const references or pointers returned from functions.

Please note that it is possible for a const member function to change static data members, global data, and the objects that pointer data members are pointing at. It is even possible to modify the object operated upon if a non-const pointer or reference to that object exists.

EXAMPLE 7.13   **Implications of** const

UselessString is a class that has not declared any const member functions.

```
class UselessString
{
   public:
      UselessString();
      UselessString(char* cp);
      UselessString(UselessString& u);

      ~UselessString();

      UselessString& operator=(UselessString& u);

      char*  cStr();
      size_t length();
      char&  operator[](size_t index);

   private:
      // ...
};
```

A consequence is that the following code, which you would expect to be legal, will not compile:

```
ostream& operator<<(ostream & o, const UselessString& s)
{
   o << s.cStr();  // Will not compile
   return o;
}
```

EXAMPLE 7.14   **Accessing objects inside a** `const` **member function**

```
class Silly
{
   public:
      explicit Silly(int val);
      void me(Silly& s) const;        // Odd function
   private:
      int  valM;
};


Silly::Silly(int val) : valM(val)
{
   // ...
}
```

The odd thing about the declaration of the function `me()` is that it takes a non-`const` parameter, which indicates that it might be changed by the function, whereas the function itself is declared as `const`. If we look at its implementation we can easily see its peculiarity.

```
void Silly::me(Silly& s) const
{
   // valM = 42;      // Error: cannot modify valM
   s.valM = 42;      // OK but odd:  s is not const
}
```

If you call the `const` member function `me()` with the object operated upon as argument, the object will be modified by the member function call despite the member function's `const`ness.

```
Silly s(7);
s.me(s);      // s.valM == 42, not 7
```

Rule 7.12 A member function that gives non-`const` access to the representation of an object must not be declared `const`.

A member function that gives non-`const` access to the representation of an object must not be declared `const` because the object has no control over possible modifications through such pointers or references. It would be awkward, if not impossible, to change constant objects using such a member function.

EXAMPLE 7.15   **Accessing characters in a string**

The following piece of code allows a string to be modified by using the indexing operator to access individual characters.

```
EmcString name = "John Bauer";
name[0] = 'B';                  // OK
```

The implementation returns a reference to a character that is part of the representation for the string and that can be assigned to. Here, the indexing operator indirectly modifies the object.

The EmcString class has overloaded operator[] with respect to constness to prevent const objects from being indirectly modified this way.

```
class EmcString
{
   public:
      EmcString(const char* cp);
      size_t length() const;
      // ...
      // Non-const version
      char& operator[](size_t index);
      // Const version
      char  operator[](size_t index) const;
      // ...
   private:
      size_t lengthM;  // Length of string
      char*  cpM;      // A pointer to the characters
};
```

The string is represented by two data members: cpM, the character array, and lengthM, the length of the string.

The implementation of the indexing operators is straightforward. They just return a reference to the character specified by the index parameter, as long as the index is within bounds.

```
char& EmcString::operator[](size_t index)
{
   assert(index < lengthM);
   return cpM[index];
}
```

The compiler would not complain if this indexing operator is declared const because it is not the pointer cpM that is modified, but only what it points at. Thus, one operator member function would have been enough, which would be a benefit for the person maintaining the class because the fewer member functions the class has, the easier it is to maintain.

From the users perspective it would be wrong to const declare the indexing operator returning a reference because that would open up the possibility that a constant string could change value. Here, the compiler's interpretation of const would not be the same as the programmer's.

```
const EmcString pioneer = "Roald Amundsen";
// pioneer[0]  = 'M';  Should NOT be legal!!
```

We want to allow each individual character of a const declared string to be accessed, but not modified. The correct way to do that is to overload the indexing operator with respect to const ness. The const member function does not return a reference so the string cannot be modified through assignment to the return value.

```
const EmcString s = "hello";

size_t length = s.length();

for (size_t j = 0; j < length; j++)
{
   // OK: Read only
   cout << "char " << j << ": " << s[j] << endl;
}
```

Rec. 7.13 Do not let const member functions change the state of the program.

A const member function promises not to change any of the data members of the object. Usually this is not enough. It should be possible to call a const member function any number of times without affecting the state of the complete program. It is therefore important that a const member function refrains from changing static data members, global data, or other objects to which the object has a pointer or reference. Objects often put some parts of their representation in separate objects and instead have data members that are pointers to these objects. As a complicating factor, the value of a data member may not be part of the state of the object. It could be a value that was very costly to calculate and therefore cached in an internal data member for efficiency reasons.

If `const` member functions fulfill their promise not to change the state of the program, then that makes them very useful as a reliable tool in assertions that check whether the program is in a consistent state. It should be possible to switch off assertions without changing the behavior of the program, so obviously `const` member functions must behave as promised.

Overloading and Default Arguments

Overloading and default arguments in C++ are two straightforward but powerful extensions to C. By avoiding a few pitfalls, you can use them to greatly reduce the complexity of a system.

RULES AND RECOMMENDATIONS

Rule 7.14   All variants of an overloaded member function should be used for the same purpose and have similar behavior.

Rec. 7.15   If you overload one of a closely related set of operators, you should overload the whole set and preserve the same invariants that exist for built-in types.

Rule 7.16   In a derived class, if you need to override one of a set of the base class's overloaded virtual member functions, you should override the whole set or use using-declarations to bring all the functions in the base class into the scope of the derived class.

Rule 7.17   Supply default arguments with the function's declaration in the header file, not with the function's definition in the implementation file.

See Also   Rec. 13.4: Overloaded functions replace functions with an unspecified number of arguments.

Rec. 10.6–Rec. 10.7: Specifying behavior of member functions.

Rule 7.14 All variants of an overloaded member function should be used for the same purpose and have similar behavior.

Different member functions can be used for essentially the same purpose. By giving all member functions the same name, you can make this fact explicit to the user of a class. This is called function name overloading.

Using function name overloading for any other purpose than to group closely related member functions is not recommended and would be very confusing.

EXAMPLE 7.16   **Overloaded member functions**

When working with strings, we sometimes want to know how many occurrences of a character or a substring it contains. The string class EmcString overloads the name contains for both these operations.

```
EmcString cosmonaut("Yury Gagarin");

char a = 'a';
bool aValue = cosmonaut.contains(a);
// aValue == true

EmcString ury("ury");
bool uryValue = cosmonaut.contains(ury);
// uryValue == true
```

If you give the member functions the same name, the code will be more readable because only one name, contains, must be remembered by the programmer.

Different versions of contains should also have the same behavior.

Rec. 7.15 If you overload one of a closely related set of operators, you should overload the whole set and preserve the same invariants that exist for built-in types.

If used correctly, operator overloading can improve the readability of the code. This is the case for classes that represent mathematical quantities such as complex numbers and for classes that replace arrays or pointers.

C++ programmers expect that all operators in a set of closely related operators are available. For example, if a class provides == for comparing two objects of the class, it should also provide

!=. In general, many relationships between operators can be described as a set of invariants. For example, if a and b are ints and if a != b is true, this implies that !(a == b) is also true. The same property should hold if a and b are objects of a class.

The general recommendation is that if you overload operators, provide all operators in a closely related set of operators and preserve the invariants that are valid for built-in types.

EXAMPLE 7.17   **Operator overloading**

If a class provides copy assignment and operator==(), two objects are expected to be equal after assigning one of them to the other.

```
Int x = 42;
Int y = 0;
x = y;
// x == y should be true
```

If a class provides the comparison operators <, <=, >, and >=, we expect that an object can either be lesser than, greater than, or equal to another object. For example, if we have a member function max that returns the largest of two operands, it should not matter what operator is used in the implementation.

```
Int max(Int x, Int y)
{
    if (x > y) // could use: < instead
    {
        // We also expect that:
        // y < x
        return x;
    }
    else
    {
        // We also expect that:
        // x <= y
        return y;
    }
}
```

It can be useful to preserve an invariant by using an operator member function in the implementation of another closely related operator member function. You could say the invariant is the implementation because it defines how to implement an operator function in terms of another overloaded operator function.

EXAMPLE 7.18   **Implementation of closely related operators**

EmcString overloads operator ==() and operator !=(). The implementation of operator!=() compares two strings and returns true if they are not equal.

```
bool EmcString::operator!=(const EmcString& s) const
{
   if (lengthM != s.lengthM)
   // Different lengths means that strings are different
   {
      return true;
   }
   else
   {
      return (strcmp(cpM, s.cpM) != 0);
   }
}
```

To check whether two strings are equal, we can simply negate the result of operator !=(). Thus, less code is needed to implement operator ==().

```
bool EmcString::operator==(const EmcString& s) const
{
   return !(*this != s);   // operator!= used here
}
```

Rule 7.16 In a derived class, if you need to override one of a set of the base class's overloaded virtual member functions, you should override the whole set or use using-declarations to bring all the functions in the base class into the scope of the derived class.

Mixing overloading and inheritance can be tricky. A problem is that in a derived class, if you override only one of the overloaded virtual functions in the base class, then the functions not overridden will be hidden for all users of the derived class.

Both virtual and nonvirtual member functions can be hidden. A hidden member function can be called only when the object is accessed through a base class pointer or reference, or when the name is qualified with the base class name.

Hidden member functions will make the code more difficult to understand. The same expression could mean different things depending on how the object is accessed. Implicit conversions must be taken in consideration and the programmer must know what versions of the overloaded function are hidden for both base classes and the actual class.

EXAMPLE 7.19   **Hiding member functions**

```
class Base
{
   public:
      // ...
      void f(char);
      void f(int);
      virtual void v(char);
      virtual void v(int);
};
```

Derived inherits Base and provides some of the overloaded functions.

```
// NOT RECOMMENDED

class Derived : public Base
{
   public:
      Derived();
      // ...
      void f(int);
      virtual void v(char);
};
```

Different member functions will be called depending on how Derived is accessed. For example, if v uses f for its implementation, the result could be surprising.

```
void Derived::v(char c)
{
   f(c);       // calls Derived::f(int), not Base::f(char)
   v((int)c); // recursive call to Derived::v(char)
}
```

If the object is accessed within the scope of Base or through a Base pointer or reference, the result of overload resolution will be different.

```
Derived d;
Base& bref = d;
char c = 'c';

bref.f(c);       // calls Base::f(char)
bref.v(c);       // calls Derived::v(char)
bref.v((int)c);  // calls Base::v(int)
```

It is not always wrong to hide member functions. A good example is a nonvirtual comparison member function that takes a reference to another object as argument. It can be difficult to compare objects of different types. You will need to use runtime type checking or define the comparison entirely in terms of virtual functions. In a derived class, if you know how to compare two objects of that class efficiently, you may want to hide the more general comparison function so that it is used only when operating on base class pointers or references.

If the member function had been declared `virtual`, the derived class could have replaced it with a more efficient version.

A virtual member function should be overridden to replace the base class implementation, not to hide any names in the base class. The natural thing is to make all inherited virtual member functions that are accessible in the base class also accessible in the derived class. It would be very strange if different virtual member functions were called depending on how the object is accessed.

If your compiler does not implement namespaces, you will have to either reimplement the member function or use an old-style access specification.

EXAMPLE 7.20   **Inheriting overloaded virtual member functions**

Suppose the template `EmcBoundedCollection<T>` inherits from `EmcCollection<T>`. Objects of the same derived class can be compared more efficiently than objects of different classes. This is why the member function `isEqual` is overloaded in the derived class, but to avoid surprises the base class version is also made accessible.

```
// Stores any number of values

template <class T>
class EmcCollection
{
   public:
      // ...
      virtual bool isEqual(const EmcCollection<T>&) const;
      bool operator==(const EmcCollection<T>&) const;
};
```

In a derived class it is OK to hide the nonvirtual `operator==()`,
but not `isEqual()`.

```
// Stores a limited number of values

template <class T>
class EmcBoundedCollection : public EmcCollection<T>
{
   public:
      // ...
      using EmcCollection<T>::isEqual;
      virtual bool
         isEqual(const EmcBoundedCollection<T>&) const;
      bool
         operator==(const EmcBoundedCollection<T>&) const;
};
```

EXAMPLE 7.21   **Old-style access specification**

```
// Not recommended

template <class T>
class EmcBoundedCollection : public EmcCollection<T>
{
   public:
      // ...
      // Old-style access specification
      EmcCollection<T>::isEqual;
      virtual bool
         isEqual(const EmcBoundedCollection<T>&) const;
      bool
         operator==(const EmcBoundedCollection<T>&) const;
};
```

Rule 7.17 Supply default arguments with the function's declaration in the header file, not with the function's definition in the implementation file.

Default arguments are a surprisingly complex area of C++. For example, it is possible to redeclare a function several times with different default arguments. We firmly believe that it is best to use default arguments only with the declaration of a function in the header file, not to make functions simpler to call in the implementation file. Such tricks tend to make the code more difficult to understand.

Think of a member function with default arguments as a substitute for a set of overloaded member functions. All such overloaded functions should be declared in the class definition, which means that you should not add default arguments outside that scope of the class, even if the language allows.

EXAMPLE 7.22   **Adding default arguments**

```
void f(int x, int y = 2);

// 50 lines of declarations later

void f(int x = 1, int y); // NOT RECOMMENDED
```

If you call f without specifying any arguments, the default arguments will be used.

```
f();      // calls f(1,2)
```

EXAMPLE 7.23   **Default arguments for a member function**

```
// RanDraw generates pseudo-random numbers

class RanDraw
{
   public:
      enum RanType {Fast, Good};
      RanDraw( double limit, int seed, RanType t = Good );
      // Default argument for t in class definition

      // ...
};
```

```
RanDraw::RanDraw(double limit, int seed, RanType t)
// No default arguments outside class definition
// ...
{
    // ...
}
```

Conversion Functions

It can be difficult to understand C++ code that uses implicit type conversions between otherwise unrelated types. Your classes can be designed to prevent such code by removing one-argument constructors and conversion functions.

RULES AND RECOMMENDATIONS

Rec. 7.18   One-argument constructors should be declared `explicit`.

Rec. 7.19   **Do not use conversion functions.**

See Also

Rec. 6.1–Rec. 6.3: A more general discussion about conversions.

Rec. 15.13: If your compiler does not support `explicit`.

Rec. 7.18 One-argument constructors should be declared `explicit`.

Implicit type conversions are bad because the behavior of existing code can change when new such conversions are added, and it is difficult to know what function is called when looking at the code.

If an object of a type is passed as an argument to a function, it is natural to expect to find a function taking that type as a parameter. If implicit type conversions are used, it is no longer that easy. A programmer must also check all implicit type conversions for the argument type in order to find out which function is actually called. This search can be quite difficult to do manually because some conversions might be defined by an otherwise unrelated class. It is best to avoid implicit type conversions and to prevent the client from depending on them.

By default, all one-argument constructors can be used for implicit type conversions. All one-argument constructors should therefore be declared as `explicit` to prevent them from being called implicitly. The keyword `explicit` is a recent addition to the C++ language and may not yet be supported by your compiler.

EXAMPLE 7.24   **One-argument constructor**

```
class Other
{
   public:
       explicit Other(const Any& a);
       // No implicit conversion from Any
       // ...
};
```

Because the class `Other` declares the constructor as `explicit`, the type must be specified when using an `Any` object instead of an `Other` object.

```
void foo(const Other& o);

Any any;
// foo(any);          // Would not compile
foo(Other(any));      // OK
```

Rec. 7.19 Do not use conversion functions. Conversion functions introduce an implicit conversion from a class to another type. You should avoid them and instead use ordinary functions to get a value of another type.

EXAMPLE 7.25   **How to avoid conversion operator functions**

Our string class `EmcString` provides a member function `cStr()` for the purpose of returning the string representation as a `const char*`.

```
class EmcString
{
   public:
       // ...
       const char* cStr() const;
       // conversion to const char*
       // ...
};
```

```
void log(const char* cp);

EmcString magicPlace("Ngoro-Ngoro crater at dusk");

log(magicPlace.cStr());
// Explicit conversion from String to const char*
```

chapter eight

new and delete

The operators `new` and `delete` are the C++ way of dynamically allocating and deallocating objects. Their use is quite error prone, but many problems can be avoided by following a few basic rules and recommendations.

Rule 8.1 `delete` should be used only with `new`.

Rule 8.2 `delete []` should be used only with `new []`.

It is important to understand how memory is managed in C++. You should understand what happens when an object is created with `new` and what happens when the `delete` operator destroys it.

Allocation and deallocation of free store objects are done in steps:

- If a single object is allocated, `operator new` is called to allocate memory, and then the constructor is called to initialize the object.
- If an array of objects is allocated, `operator new[]` is called to allocate memory for the whole array, and then the constructor is called for each element of the array.
- When a single object is deleted, the destructor for the object is called first, and then `operator delete` is called to free the memory occupied by the object.
- When an array of objects is deleted, the destructor for each element of the array object is called first, and then `operator delete[]` is called to free the memory occupied by the array.

Because different functions are used for allocation and deallocation of single objects and arrays of objects, you must use the correct `delete` expression when a pointer is deleted. If not, the wrong function will be called to release the memory occupied by the object.

The reason that different functions are called is that an implementation should be able to use the algorithms that are best suited for either case. If different algorithms are used, the memory will not be properly released if the wrong function is called, and the program will probably crash.

EXAMPLE 8.1   Allocate and deallocate a free store object

Because `EmcString` does not overload `operator new` or `operator delete`, the default functions for memory allocation will be called.

```
EmcString* sp = new EmcString("Hello");
// Calls ::operator new()
delete sp;
// Calls ::operator delete()
```

```
const size_t arraySize = 5;

EmcString* sa = new EmcString[arraySize];
// Calls ::operator new[]()
delete [] sa;
// Calls ::operator delete[]()
```

Rule 8.3 Do not access a pointer or reference to a deleted object.

You must decide what to do with your pointer after you have deleted the object assigned to it. A pointer that has been used as argument to a `delete` expression should not be used again unless you have given it a new value, because the language does not define what should happen if you access a deleted object. You could assign the pointer to 0 or a new valid object. Otherwise, you get a "dangling" pointer.

EXAMPLE 8.2   **Dangerous access to a deleted object**

The following code is legal, but the behavior is undefined.

```
EmcString* sp = new EmcString("Hello");
delete sp;
cout << *sp << endl;       // No: Undefined behavior !!
```

Rec. 8.4 Do not delete `this`.

You should also avoid deleting the `this` pointer. It is potentially dangerous to do so, and your code will be more difficult to understand.

It is dangerous to provide a member function that deletes `this`, because it is possible that the `this` pointer must be accessed when returning from the function.

You should not try to delete an object allocated on the stack with such a member function. A common trick is to declare the destructor as either `private` or `protected` to prevent objects on the stack from being created.

EXAMPLE 8.3   **Objects that commit suicide**

```
class W
{
    public:
        W();
        void goAway();
        static void foo();
        void bar();
        // ...
    protected:
        ~W();
};
```

Objects of the class W can be created only with new because the class has a protected destructor. For that reason, it is not possible to delete the object outside the scope of the class. Instead, the member function goAway() deletes the object.

```
void W::goAway()
{
    delete this;      // No!!
}
```

```
W* w = new W;
w->goAway();
```

After the call to goAway(), what happens if you try to use the pointer is undefined.

```
w->foo();             // May crash !!!
w->bar();             // May crash !!!
```

Rec. 8.5 If you overload operator new for a class, you should have a corresponding overloaded operator delete.

Objects can be allocated with many different new expressions. The result of a new expression is either a null pointer or a pointer to an object with a lifetime that is determined by the programmer. When the object is no longer needed, some code is needed to properly return the memory and perhaps other resources allocated by the object. Deleting a pointer to the object is not always the right thing to do because memory could have been allocated by some means other than operator new(size_t).

For example, it is possible to provide additional placement arguments in a new expression. The function that allocates storage for such an object is also called a placement operator new.

EXAMPLE 8.4   **Placement new**

A common form of placement new that is part of the standard library takes a memory address as argument.

```
const int maxSize = 100;

// get storage for object
// assumption: sizeof(A) < 100
void* storage = (void*)new char[maxSize];

// call placement new to create object
A* ap1 = new (storage) A();
```

Deleting a pointer to such an object is not recommended, but the destructor should always be called. It is possible and correct to call the destructor explicitly in this situation.

```
// Use ap1
ap1->~A(); // call destructor, not delete

// reuse storage: sizeof(B) < 100
B* bp1 = new (storage) B();
// ...
delete [] (char*)storage;
```

It is possible to overload operator new, operator delete, operator new[], and operator delete [] for a class. If we want to customize memory management for a class this is the correct thing to do.

The interaction between exception handling and customized memory management must be understood to avoid memory-related errors.

If an exception is thrown by a constructor for an object created with new, the runtime system is responsible for returning the memory allocated for the object. The client has no way of doing this because a pointer to the object is not available until the object has been fully constructed. For this to work, the runtime system must know how to correctly deallocate objects created by different new expressions.

The scope of the operator new used by the new expression is searched for a matching operator delete. A declaration of an `operator delete` matches the declaration of an `operator new` when it has the same number of parameters and all parameter types except the first are identical. The runtime system then calls the matching `operator delete` to deallocate a partially constructed object.

Until recently it was not possible to provide additional arguments to `operator delete` and `operator delete[]`, but now it is both possible and recommended to overload these member functions if a class has its own memory management. If not, the program could crash before an exception handler is given the chance to handle the exception, and there is also the risk of memory leaks.

If the compiler does not support this rather new language feature, one deallocation function that can be used with all different allocation functions is an alternative to overloaded deallocation functions, but then additional arguments to the `new` expression will not be available when the deallocation function is called. This makes it difficult to customize memory management when exception handling, but not placement delete, is supported by the compiler.

EXAMPLE 8.5   **Class with customized memory management**

The class A has customized memory management. The idea is to have a memory pool, here represented by class `Pool<A>`, that can be used for the allocation of objects. When using the memory pool, the programmer only has to worry about the lifetime of the `Pool<A>` object and not the individual objects. An additional placement argument of the type `Pool<A>&` is provided to allow the user to allocate objects this way.

```
class BadArgument
{
    public:
        explicit BadArgument(int);
        // ...
};

class A
{
    public:
        A();
        A(int) throw (BadArgument);
        ~A();
        // ...
```

```
          void* operator new(size_t size);
          void* operator new[](size_t size);
          void* operator new(size_t size, Pool<A>& p);
          void* operator new[](size_t size, Pool<A>& p);

          void  operator delete(void* vp);
          void  operator delete[](void* vp);
          void  operator delete(void* vp, Pool<A>& p);
          void  operator delete[](void* vp, Pool<A>& p);
          // ...
      };
```

A has a constructor that sometimes throws an exception. If an exception is thrown the correct operator delete() will be called.

```
A::A(int i) throw (BadArgument)
{
   // ...
   if (i == 42) throw BadArgument(42);
}


A* createA(int i)
{
   // throws exception if i == 42
   return new A(i);
   // if exception is thrown, call
   // A::operator delete(void*)
}


A* createA(int i, Pool<A>& memoryPool)
{
   // throws exception if i == 42
   return new (memoryPool) A(i);
   // if exception is thrown, call
   // A::operator delete(void*, Pool<A>& p)
}
```

Rec. 8.6 Customize the memory management for a class if memory management is an unacceptably large part of the allocation and deallocation of free store objects of that class.

When should a class customize its memory management? Different memory management algorithms have different performance characteristics. When using a general algorithm, both the size and location of memory blocks must be stored and updated by the functions. A customized allocator that manages memory blocks of only one size does less bookkeeping and is therefore faster.

Some objects are often created in large numbers on the free store. Sometimes the memory management of such objects can be a large part of the overall time spent on allocation of such objects. In these cases it can be well worth the effort to customize the memory management for such a class. Programs can be made to run five times faster by such customized memory management, so this can be a good idea if your program runs unacceptably slow.

chapter nine
9

Static Objects

Global objects, static data members, file scope objects, and local variables declared `static` are variables with static storage duration. A strategy for initialization of objects with static storage duration is needed to avoid accessing uninitialized objects.

RULES AND RECOMMENDATIONS

Rec. 9.1   Objects with static storage duration should be declared only within the scope of a class, function, or anonymous namespace.

Rec. 9.2   Document how static objects are initialized.

See Also   Rec. 1.4–Rec. 1.5: Namespaces.

Rec. 9.1 Objects with static storage duration should be declared only within the scope of a class, function, or anonymous namespace.

Static objects make it possible to access an object inside a function without having to pass along a pointer or reference to it. Many objects can use the same object without each storing a pointer to the object, which can save space and sometimes make the code less complex.

There are also many disadvantages of giving access to static objects. Any function that has access to a static object could use it, which means that it can be costly and difficult to maintain code with many static objects.

In addition they can complicate multithreaded applications because it is necessary to protect static objects so that their states do not become invalid if two threads modify an object at the same time.

We recommend that you limit the scope of a static object to a class, a function, or an unnamed namespace. By doing so, you can know in advance where a static object is accessed.

Encapsulate access to static objects as much as possible. If you can declare a static object within a function, you should do so. Such objects are guaranteed to have been initialized before the first use of the function.

The choice between a static data member and a static object within an unnamed namespace is not as obvious. The latter alternative is more flexible regarding scope, but the first choice allows you to put the implementation of a class in many different files.

Unnamed namespaces allow you to use the same name for many different objects with static storage duration. For example, it is common to have a static string to identify each implementation file that a program uses.

Experienced C++ programmers should know that objects within unnamed namespaces replace static objects in file scope. The language has changed, and there is now no guarantee that static objects in file scope will be supported in the future.

EXAMPLE 9.1   **Function local static object**

```
int randomValue(int seed)
{
   static int oldValue = seed;
   // calculate new value
   return oldValue;
}
```

EXAMPLE 9.2   **Static data member**

A singleton class is a class with only one instance. It is common to store a static data member that is a pointer to that object. This gives static member functions access to the object.

The pointer cannot be local to a function because many static member functions need access to the object.

```
class EmcSingleton
{
   public:
      static EmcSingleton* instance();
      static void create(int i = 0);
      // ...
   private:
      // private constructors
      EmcSingleton(int i);
      // ...
      static EmcSingleton* instanceM;
};

EmcSingleton* EmcSingleton::instanceM = 0;

void EmcSingleton::create(int i)
{
   instanceM = new EmcSingleton(i);
}

EmcSingleton* EmcSingleton::instance()
{
   if (! instanceM) create();
   return instanceM;
}
```

EXAMPLE 9.3   Unnamed namespace

```
// myfile.cc

namespace
{
   // sccsid is not visible to other files
   const char sccsid[] = "@(#)myfile.cc ...";
}

// ...
```

EXAMPLE 9.4   Static objects in the file scope

```
// Not recommended if your compiler allows you to
// have unnamed namespaces

static const char sccsid[] = "@(#)myfile.cc ...";
```

Rec. 9.2 Document how static objects are initialized.

Static objects defined in different implementation files are initialized in an order that is not specified by the language.

This is a problem when static objects are used by constructors used to initialize other static objects. Programs that depend on any particular order could work on one platform and crash on another. Ignoring the problem is asking for trouble.

EXAMPLE 9.5 **Access to a static object inside a constructor**

Suppose a constructor writes a message to `cout`. If the `iostream` library had not provided a method for safe initialization of `cout`, constructors for initialization of such static objects would be dangerous to use.

```
#include <iostream.h>

class EmcLog
{
    public:
        EmcLog(ostream& out);
        // ...
};

EmcLog::EmcLog(ostream& out)
// ...
{
    out << "Creating log" << endl;
    // ...
}

// cout must have been initialized before initializing
// theLog.

EmcLog theLog(cout); // static object
```

To avoid surprises, the programmer should document under what circumstances static objects, and the functions and classes that depend on them, can be used. In order to do that, the programmer must understand how static objects are initialized and how to control the initialization order.

You should always try to declare static objects initialized by constructors inside their corresponding access functions. These objects are initialized when control passes through the function for the first time. This solution does not require the client to do anything special before using the function.

If using such access functions is not possible, consider using static pointers instead of objects because that allows you to control how the objects are initialized. The simple rule is that before you use a function or a class that needs to use the static pointers to access objects, you must call a function that creates the objects bound to them.

In what way can that help? Because you do not depend on any implementation-defined order, your program will be more portable. Another desirable property is that the client can control when the initialization function is called.

An initialization function often has a corresponding finalization function that should be called before the program is terminated. By having an initialization class that manages resources, the programmer can automatically get finalization by putting a call to the finalization function inside the destructor.

There are rules for how static objects within the same translation unit are initialized. If two static objects are defined within the same translation unit, but outside the scope of a function, their initialization order will be the same as the order of their definitions.

Note: This is the opposite to the rules for nonstatic data members, where the declaration order, not the order of initializers, determines initialization order.

EXAMPLE 9.6   Initialization order of static objects

```
// sccsid initialized before release.

namespace
{
    const char sccsid[] = "@(#)myfile.cc ...";
    const char release[] = "@(#)Emc Class Library, 1.2";
};
```

You can take advantage of this order when classes and functions require initialization. Many class libraries provide file local initialization objects within their header files to make sure that the classes can be used without trouble. This is what the `iostream` library does. This solution is safe, but costly in terms of performance and memory. Many small objects with constructors will be created before you enter `main` and the number of objects will increase as the number of implementation files used to build the program gets bigger.

For some applications this is not acceptable, so you should avoid such general solutions. It is better to let users control when and where the library is initialized. Only if you want to access functions that depend on static objects before entering `main()` must you declare a static initialization object.

EXAMPLE 9.7   Initialization object

Suppose you have a class `EmcObject` that requires initialization. The class provides a nested class `Initor` for that purpose. The implementation of `Initor` uses two member functions provided by `EmcObject`, `initialize`, and `finalize`, that do the actual initialization and finalization of the class. An initialization object should be created before `EmcObject` objects are operated on.

```
class EmcObject
{
  public:
      // ...
      class Initor
      {
        public:
            Initor();
            ~Initor();
        private:
            static int refcountM;
      };
      friend class Initor;

  private:
      static void initialize();
      static void finalize();

      // ...
};
```

The implementation must prevent a class from being initialized or finalized more than once. All `EmcObject::Initor` objects share a reference count that is updated each time an object is created. This is a common technique for safe initialization of static objects. By checking the value, we make sure that the class is initialized and finalized only once.

```
// EmcObject.cc

int EmcObject::Initor::refcountM = 0;

EmcObject::Initor::Initor()
{
   if (refcountM == 0) EmcObject::initialize();
   refcountM++;
}

EmcObject::Initor::~Initor()
{
   refcountM--;
   if (refcountM == 0) EmcObject::finalize();
}
```

Before the client uses the class, an `EmcObject::Initor` object is created inside an unnamed namespace. Thus, there is no risk of name clashes if more than one object with that name is created.

```
// client code

namespace
{
   EmcObject::Initor initor;    // initializes EmcObject
   // ...
}

// more code ...
```

Object-Oriented Programming

In this chapter we discuss rules and recommendations concerning the most important parts of object-oriented programming: encapsulation, dynamic binding, inheritance, and software contracts.

Encapsulation

There are many aspects of encapsulation. For any data member, the source code that may access it directly must be limited to a part of the program that can be deduced from inspecting the class definition only. The main idea is that users should not be affected by modifications to the class representation as long as the class interface is unchanged.

RULES AND RECOMMENDATIONS

Rule 10.1   Declare data members private.

Rec. 10.2   If a member function returns a pointer or reference, you should document how it should be used and for how long it is valid.

See Also   Rec. 5.5, Rule 5.6, Rec. 5.7: Initialization of data members.

Rule 7.7: Return value of copy assignment operator.

Rule 10.1 Declare data
members private.

Public data members should be avoided. By having only private data members, it is possible to know in advance what code modifies data members. This makes it less likely that the state of the object will be corrupted by mistake.

We want to avoid having users depend on the representation of the object. With public data members, it is difficult to predict how much code must be modified when the representation changes. There is also always a risk that the user might modify data members in a way you did not anticipate, creating bugs that are hard to find.

Imagine how hard it would be to maintain a class with public data members. Many bugs would probably be the user's own fault, even though the program crashes inside member functions of the class. By declaring data members private, you reduce the effort it takes to maintain the class.

It is also impossible to change the name or type of public data members because that would immediately break all code using them. If you avoid public data members, then the internal representation of a class can be changed without users of the class having to modify their code.

We also recommend that you avoid protected data members because member functions of derived classes have the same kind of unrestricted and possibly dangerous access to protected data members as other functions have to public data members. Some might argue that constant members could be declared protected without risk because these cannot be modified. Even here a member function interface is slightly better because it makes the base class and the derived class more loosely coupled.

Rec. 10.2 If a member
function returns a
pointer or reference, you
should document how it
should be used and for
how long it is valid.

Private data members are a good step toward encapsulation, but they are not enough. We must always document ownership and lifetime of objects to which we return pointers or references, and also any restrictions on how we use such pointers or references.

It is not always wrong to return a pointer or reference to an object, but if we have a badly designed class interface, we might use the object in a way that was not intended.

It is always unwise to give uncontrolled access to data that are part of an object's state. If such access is necessary, it is important that the user know how to use the class correctly. A good design principle is to have as few limitations as possible on how to use a pointer or reference returned from a function.

EXAMPLE 10.1   **Assigning to a string element**

When assigning to an element of a string or an array, it is easier to read and understand the code if we use the same syntax as for built-in arrays.

EmcString has overloaded [] to allow assignment of individual elements of the string. This operator returns a reference to an array element that can be assigned to.

```
EmcString s = "Hello";
s[0] = 'h';                   // Better than: s.set(0,'h');
```

The reference is only guaranteed to be valid as long as the string does not change. To store the reference in a local variable is to ask for trouble.

```
char& s0 = s[0];         // No, should not keep reference
s0 = 'h';                // OK, but not recommended
s = "Goodbye";
s0 = 'g';                // Now, you are on thin ice!
```

Sometimes a function returns a pointer or a reference to an object that must be managed by the user. Typically the user must delete the object in order to prevent a memory leak. If a function transfers ownership of an object to which it returns a pointer or reference, then this must always be documented. A good strategy is to use a naming convention to make it obvious to the user when the object must be deleted by the user. You could give such functions a name that starts with new, make, or create.

Dynamic Binding

C++ allows you to write code that depends only on a base class interface. It is possible to bind base class pointers or references to objects of derived classes and to operate on them without knowing their exact type. This makes it possible to add new derived classes without having to change the code that operates on them. This makes programs easier to adapt to changing user requirements.

Here we want to explain how and when to use dynamic binding in your programs.

RULES AND RECOMMENDATIONS

Rec. 10.3   **Selection statements (if-else and switch) should be used when the control flow depends on an object's value; dynamic binding should be used when the control flow depends on the object's type.**

See Also   Rule 4.1, Rec. 4.2–Rec. 4.5: Writing if and switch statements.

Rec. 10.3 Selection statements (if-else and switch) should be used when the control flow depends on an object's value; dynamic binding should be used when the control flow depends on the object's type.

Heavy use of the selection statements if-else and switch might be an indication of a poor design. Selection statements should be used primarily when the control flow depends on the value of an object.

Selection statements are not the best choice if the control flow depends on the type of an object. If you want to have an extensible set of types that you operate on, code that uses objects of different types will be difficult and costly to maintain. Each time you need to add a new type, each selection statement must be updated with a new branch. It is best to localize selection statements to a few places in the code. However, this requires that you use inheritance and virtual member functions.

It is possible to operate on objects of derived classes without knowing their type if you call only virtual member functions declared by a public base class. Such member function calls are dynamically bound; that is, the function to call is chosen in run-time. Dynamic binding is an essential component of object-oriented programming, and we cannot overemphasize the importance of understanding this part of C++. You should try to use dynamic binding instead of selection statements as much as possible. It gives you a more flexible design because you can add classes without rewriting code that depends only on the base class interface.

EXAMPLE 10.2   Factory class

EmcCollection<T> is a base class that allows many different types of object collections to be manipulated through the same interface. It is meant only to be derived from and each derived class must override a set of pure virtual member functions.

```
template <class T>
class EmcCollection
{
   public:
      // ...

      // insert one element
      virtual void insert(const T&) = 0; // pure virtual
      // ...

};

template <class T>
ostream&
operator<<(ostream&, const EmcCollection<T>& coll);
```

EmcArrayCollection is a class template derived from EmcCollection<T> that implements the base class interface. All pure virtual member functions are overridden so that an EmcArrayCollection<T> object can be created.

```
template <class T>
class EmcArrayCollection
   : public virtual EmcCollection<T>
{
   public:
      static const size_t initialSize = 10;
      EmcArrayCollection(size_t maxsize = initialSize);
      // ...
};
```

A user of EmcCollectionFactory can create objects of classes
derived from EmcCollection<T> without explicitly including
their class definitions in the program, which makes the program
less sensitive to changes in the implementation.

```
class InvalidCollectionType : public EmcException
{
   public:
      InvalidCollectionType(int id);
      // ...
   private:
      int idM;
};
```

```
template <class T>
class EmcCollectionFactory
{
   public:

      EmcCollectionFactory();
      // ...
      enum EmcCollectionId { ArrayId = 0, /* ... */ };
      virtual EmcCollection<T>* create(int type) const
         throw(InvalidCollectionType);
      virtual EmcCollection<T>* createArray() const;
      // ...
   private:
      // ...
};
```

Each class derived from EmcCollection<T> has its own type
identifier represented as an integer. This identifier is passed to the
create member function when creating an object.

```
EmcCollection<T>*
EmcCollectionFactory<T>::create(int type) const
   throw(InvalidCollectionType)
{
   // Select behavior based on the value of type.

   switch (type)
   {
      case ArrayId:
      {
         return createArray();
      }
      // ...
      default:
      {
         throw InvalidCollectionType(type);
      }
   }
   return 0; // Never reached
}

template <class T>
EmcCollection<T>*
EmcCollectionFactory<T>::createArray() const
{
   return new EmcArrayCollection<T>();
}
```

EXAMPLE 10.3 Dynamic binding

Suppose you have created an object of the class `EmcArrayCollection<int>` with a call to `EmcCollectionFactory<int>::create()`. That object can be assigned to an `EmcCollection<int>` pointer and operated on using virtual member functions declared by the base class.

```
EmcCollectionFactory<int> factory;
EmcCollection<int>* collection =
   factory.create(EmcCollectionFactory<int>::ArrayId);

collection->insert(42);
// EmcArrayCollection<int>::insert() is called

cout << *collection << endl;
delete collection;
```

Inheritance

If you use inheritance, you need to plan in advance how the base class is meant to be used. Many base classes must have virtual destructors, but not all. Sometimes a base class should be declared virtual and sometimes not.

RULES AND RECOMMENDATIONS

Rule 10.4   A public base class must have either a public virtual destructor or a protected destructor.

Rule 10.5   If you derive from more than one base class with the same parent, that parent should be a virtual base class.

See Also   Rule 8.1–Rule 8.2: How to delete objects.

Rule 10.4 A public base class must have either a public virtual destructor or a protected destructor.

When a class appears as a public base class, derived classes should be specializations of the base class. This allows objects of derived classes to be operated on through base class pointers or references. The user can use an object without knowing its exact type if a virtual member function is called.

The destructor is a member function that in most cases should be declared `virtual`. It is necessary to declare it `virtual` in a base class if derived class objects are deleted through a base class pointer. If the destructor is not declared `virtual`, only the base class destructor will be called when an object is deleted that way. In addition, the size of the base class object, not the size of the complete object, will be passed to `operator delete()`.

However, there is a case where it is not appropriate to use virtual destructors: mix-in classes. Such a class is used to define a small part of an interface, which is inherited (mixed in) by subclasses. In these cases the destructor, and hence the possibility of a user deleting a pointer to such a mix-in base class, should normally not be part of the interface offered by the base class. It is best in these cases to have a nonvirtual, nonpublic destructor because that will prevent a user of a pointer to such a base class from claiming ownership of the object and deciding to simply delete it.

In such cases it is appropriate to make the destructor protected. This will stop users from accidentally deleting an object through a pointer to the mix-in base class, so it is no longer necessary to require the destructor to be virtual.

EXAMPLE 10.4 **Deleting a derived class object**

EmcCollection<T> has a derived class EmcArrayCollection<T> that stores an array of T objects.

```
class EmcCollection
{
   public:
      // ...
      // destructor virtual for base class
      virtual ~EmcCollection();
      // ...
};


template <class T>
class EmcArrayCollection : public virtual EmcCollection<T>
{
   public:
      // ...
      ~EmcArrayCollection();
      // ...
   private:
      size_t       indexM;
      EmcArray<T> arrayM;
      // ...
};
```

The destructor of the EmcArray<T> member must be called when the object's life ends because otherwise memory allocated for the array will not be released. It is necessary to declare the destructor virtual in the base class, if we want to be sure that the derived class object is properly deleted.

```
EmcCollectionFactory<int> factory;
EmcCollection<int>* collection =
   factory.create(EmcCollectionFactory<int>::ArrayId);
// ...
delete collection;

// 1. ~EmcArrayCollection<int>() is called
// 2. ~EmcArray<int>() is called
// 3. ~EmcCollection<int>() is called
// 4. ::operator delete(sizeof EmcArray<int>, cp)
//    is called
```

The destructor for `EmcArray` in this case would never have been called if the destructor for `EmcCollection` had not been declared `virtual`.

Multiple inheritance is a language feature that is seldom used, but it is very useful if you want to derive from classes in two different class libraries. It is then possible to have one derived class instead of many.

Each object of a derived class has an object representing each base class: a base class member. A problem with multiple inheritance is that when two base classes inherit from the same class, the default is to duplicate that base class member in the derived class, not to share it.

Why is this bad? Because you actually have two base class objects, and you cannot assign the derived class object to a pointer or reference to that base class without specifying the inheritance path.

```
class Base
{
   public:
      // ...
      void baseMemberFunction();
};
class DerivedRight : public Base
{
   // ...
};


class DerivedLeft : public Base
{
   // ...
};


class MostlyDerived : public DerivedLeft, public DerivedRight
{
   public:
      MostlyDerived();
      // ...
};

MostlyDerived mostlyDerived;
Base* bp1 = (DerivedLeft*)&mostlyDerived;
Base* bp2 = (DerivedRight*)&mostlyDerived; // bp1 != bp2
```

You cannot call a member function introduced by that base class when directly operating on objects of the derived class without explicitly qualifying the name with a base class name.

```
mostlyDerived.DerivedLeft::baseMemberFunction();
```

When inheritance is nonvirtual, all names that are introduced by the base class will be ambiguous, which is why we should avoid duplicated base classes.

It is more natural to share base class objects, but this requires each base class that appears more than once to be a virtual base class.

EXAMPLE 10.5   Virtual base class

The class `EmcLogged` allows an object to write a log message on a format that is specified by the implementation of `EmcLogged`. It is meant to be used as a base class only and is an example of a mix-in base class.

```
class EmcLogged
{
   public:
      virtual void writeClassName(ostream&) const = 0;
      virtual void writeObjectId(ostream&) const;
      virtual void writeValue(ostream&) const = 0;

      void logMessage(const char* message) const;

   protected:
      ~EmcLogged();              // mix-in base class
};
```

The class has two pure virtual member functions that must be implemented by a derived class. They are called by the nonvirtual member function `logMessage()`. This function prints a log message to a file.

Suppose we want to make it possible to write a collection to the log. We create a new class template `EmcLoggedCollection` that inherits from both `EmcCollection<T>` and `EmcLogged`, both of which are declared virtual base classes.

```
template <class T>
class EmcLoggedCollection
    : public virtual EmcCollection<T>,
      public virtual EmcLogged
{
   public:
      void writeValue(ostream&) const;

   protected:
      ~EmcLoggedCollection();
};
```

The member function `writeValue()` is implemented so that operator `<<()` is used to print a collection object. The class is abstract because it does not implement `writeClassName()`.

```
template <class T>
void EmcLoggedCollection<T>::writeValue(ostream& o) const
{
   o << *this;
}
```

Because the `EmcCollection<T>` is a virtual base class, we can mix in this behavior into another template derived from `EmcArray-Collection<T>`. Here, virtual inheritance is necessary because otherwise `EmcCollection<T>` appears as a base class more than once.

```
template <class T>
class EmcLoggedArrayCollection
    : public virtual EmcArrayCollection<T>,
      public virtual EmcLoggedCollection<T>

{
   public:
      EmcLoggedArrayCollection();
      // ...
      virtual void writeClassName(ostream&) const;

   protected:
      ~EmcLoggedArrayCollection();
};
```

`EmcLoggedArrayCollection<T>` implements its constructors and its destructor so that a log message is written when these member functions are called. We could use this class when debugging our programs.

Class hierarchy for EmcLogged ArrayCollection.

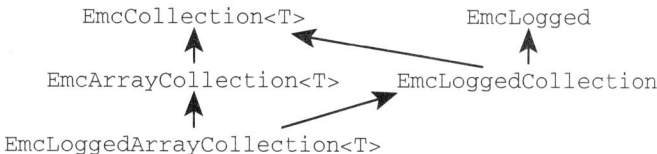

Inheritance can also be used to extend `EmcCollectionFactory`. Here, there is no need for virtual inheritance.

We create a class template `EmcLoggedCollectionFactory` that creates objects of classes that derive from `EmcLoggedCollection<T>`. The advantage of this approach is that we can trace how objects are created and deleted without changing the implementation of our existing `EmcCollection` classes. All that was required was the virtual inheritance from `EmcCollection<T>`.

```
template <class T>
class EmcLoggedCollectionFactory
    : public EmcCollectionFactory<T>
{
   public:
      virtual EmcCollection<T>* createArray() const;
};

template <class T>
EmcCollection<T>*
EmcLoggedCollectionFactory<T>::createArray() const
{
   return new EmcLoggedArrayCollection<T>();
}
```

Because we depend only on the base class interface, we need to change only the type of the factory object that is created.

```
EmcLoggedCollectionFactory<int> factory;

EmcCollection<int>* collection =
   factory.create(EmcCollectionFactory<int>::ArrayId);
```

```
collection->insert(42);
// EmcLoggedArrayCollection<int>::insert() is called

// ...
delete collection;
```

The Class Interface

When you design object-oriented systems, you must know how to describe class interfaces. Each class interface has member functions, types, and relationships to other classes that must be described in a class specification.

The class specification should describe not only how the class should be implemented, but also how it should be used. The class specification is a software contract that must be obeyed by both the user of the class and the class supplier.

It is important to distinguish this external view of objects from their representation because a class specification should not depend on any particular implementation of a class.

If a class appears as a public base class, the class specification is also valid for all its derived classes. Proper use of inheritance is important for good object-oriented design. Proper inheritance means that the interface of a public base class is also implemented correctly by derived classes. A derived class should not modify the base class interface, just extend it.

If C++ is used to describe preconditions, postconditions, and class invariants, test programs will be much easier to write and the specification will be more exact.

RULES AND RECOMMENDATIONS	Rec. 10.6	Specify classes using preconditions, postconditions, exceptions, and class invariants.
	Rec. 10.7	Use C++ to describe preconditions, postconditions, and class invariants.
	Rule 10.8	It should be possible to use a pointer or reference to an object of a derived class wherever a pointer or reference to a public base class object is used.
	Rec. 10.9	Document the interface of template parameters.

See Also Rule 11.1, Rec. 11.2: Assertions can be useful if you need to check conditions in your program.

Rec. 10.6 Specify classes using preconditions, postconditions, exceptions, and class invariants. The program operates on objects by calling member functions. We want to write correct programs, which means that we must understand how to use the objects correctly. Unless we are careful, programming errors could result in unexpected runtime errors that terminate the program. We should also try to minimize the chance that a program relies on undocumented features.

A class specification should be the programmer's primary description of a class, which prevents us from making mistakes. The class specification should give more information than you can deduce by reading the code, so we recommend that you provide preconditions, postconditions, and exceptions for each member function.

The user must know under what conditions a member function can be called and whether it has been implemented correctly.

The user's obligations are described as member function preconditions that describe the circumstances under which a member function can be called.

Preconditions are conditions that should be valid on entry to a member function. Their purpose is to prevent an object from being used incorrectly.

The supplier's obligations are described as class invariants and member function postconditions. The class invariant describes conditions that are valid for all objects of the class.

Postconditions are conditions that should be valid on exit from a member function; their purpose is to specify how the state of an object is modified by a member function.

EXAMPLE 10.6 **Preconditions and postconditions**

A stack is a classic example of an abstract data type with preconditions and postconditions, represented here by the class `EmcIntStack`.

Initially a stack is empty. After you have pushed an element onto the stack, the stack is no longer empty. It is possible to push an element onto the stack as long as the stack is not full and to pop an element as long as the stack is not empty.

We can express this knowledge as preconditions and postconditions of the corresponding member functions in the class.

```
class EmcIntStack
{
   public:
      // ...
      int  empty() const;
      int  full() const;
      int  top() const;
      void push(int i);
      int  pop();

   private:
      // ...
};

void EmcIntStack::push(int i)
{
   // Precondition:  ! full()
   // ...
   // Postcondition: ! empty()
}

int  EmcIntStack::pop()
{
   // Precondition: ! empty()
   // ...
   // Postcondition: ! full()
}
```

Preconditions and postconditions should always be valid, but what if they are not? The implementation of the member function should be written with the assumption that the precondition is valid, so it is the code that uses a class that must be modified if a precondition is not valid. This means that it is sometimes necessary to check the precondition before operating on the object.

On the other hand, the implementation of a class must be modified if a postcondition is not valid because implementation must make the postcondition valid.

EXAMPLE 10.7   **Using a member function with a precondition**

```
EmcString makeString(const EmcIntStack& stack)
{
   EmcString returnValue;
   EmcIntStack copy(stack);
   ostrstream out;

   while (! copy.empty())
   // loop condition makes precondition valid
   {
      out << copy.pop();   // Precondition: ! copy.empty()
   }

   out << ends;
   char* buf = out.str();
   returnValue = buf;
   delete [] buf;
   return returnValue;
}
```

A class invariant could be seen as a set of conditions that must be valid for all objects of a class outside its member functions. Each public member function must leave the object in a state where the class invariant is valid. This means that the invariant should also be valid on entry to all public member functions.

Preconditions, postconditions, and invariants are not part of the C++ language. Some languages, such as Eiffel, have explicit language support that allows the programmer to specify preconditions, postconditions, and invariants using the programming language, but C++ does not have that.

EXAMPLE 10.8   **Class with an invariant**

We could assume that the lengths of all EmcString objects are greater than or equal to 0 and equal to the length of the 0-terminated string returned from cStr(). This assumption is not correct, however, because this string class overloads [], which allows us to assign a 0-character in the middle of the string. When specifying class invariants, we must make sure that it is difficult to break the invariant because that would make the class specification useless.

```
class EmcString
{
   public:
      // ...
      const char* cStr() const;
      // cStr() returns 0-terminated string
      size_t      length() const;
      char&       operator[](size_t index);
      // ...

      // Invariant:
      // length() >= 0

      // Not always true:
      // length() == ::strlen(cStr())
};
```

Rec. 10.7 Use C++ to describe preconditions, postconditions, and class invariants.

If it is possible, preconditions, postconditions, and class invariants should be expressed as C++ expressions. Otherwise, the specification is open to human interpretation and will only rarely be an accurate description of the class. But there are a few exceptions. Some conditions cannot be checked inside a program or are too costly to check.

If you use C++ to express conditions, and if the conditions can be checked outside the scope of the class, test programs are easy to write. A good test program verifies both the specification and the implementation of a class. A program should behave the same with and without such checks, so inside such expressions it is essential only to observe properties of objects, not to modify them.

Normally, this means that the only member functions that should be called in such expressions are public accessors because these should not modify the state of any objects. Constants and functions that do not modify any objects can also be used.

EXAMPLE 10.9   Using comments to specify a class template

```
// EmcCollection is an abstract template class
// that allows a user to add, remove, and search
// for objects within an arbitrary collection.

// REQUIRE(e), e is a precondition
// ENSURE(e), e is a postcondition
// throw(e), e is an exception type that an
// implementation may throw
```

```
template <class T>
class EmcCollection
{
   public:

      virtual ~EmcCollection();

      // insert one element
      virtual void      insert(const T&) = 0;
      // REQUIRE(! isFull())
      // ENSURE(! isEmpty())
      // throw(bad_alloc)

      // remove all elements
      virtual void      clear() = 0;
      // ENSURE(isEmpty())

      // ...

      // Remove one element
      virtual T         remove() = 0;
      // REQUIRE(!isEmpty())
      // ENSURE(!isFUll())

      // ...
};
```

The member function insert() has a precondition: The collection must not be full when you insert an object. It is possible to check this condition by calling the accessor member function isFull(). It also has a postcondition: The collection must not be empty after an element has been inserted.

EXAMPLE 10.10   Checking a precondition

```
EmcCollectionFactory<int> factory;
EmcCollection<int>* collection =
   factory.create(EmcCollectionFactory<int>::ArrayId);

if (! collection->isFull())
{
   collection->insert(42);
   // ...
}
```

Rule 10.8 It should be possible to use a pointer or reference to an object of a derived class wherever a pointer or reference to a public base class object is used.

A class inherits from another class in order to reuse the implementation or the class interface. Public inheritance makes it possible to write code that depends only on the base class interface, not on the implementation. Public inheritance should be used only if derived class objects are supposed to be operated on through base class pointers or references.

You should reconsider the way inheritance is used, if it is dangerous to call inherited member functions for a derived class object. Such member functions can be called either directly by the base class implementation, or indirectly when the object is accessed through a base class pointer or reference.

Substitutability is a property of derived classes that allows you to use objects of these classes without changing code that depends on the base class interface only. If a virtual member function has a precondition and a postcondition, then these must be valid for all implementations of the class interface. If they are not, the derived class should not inherit the base class.

EXAMPLE 10.11   **Substitutability**

```
// insertObject() works for any class with
// EmcCollection<T> as public base class.

template <class T>
bool insertObject(EmcCollection<T>& c, const T& element)
// throw (bad_alloc)
{
   // return false if insertion fails, true otherwise

   if (! c.isFull())
   {
      c.insert(element);
      return true;
   }
   return false;
}
```

Note: It is worth noting that this function does not have an exception specification. The main reason is that we want to allow any EmcCollection instantiations to use this function. An exception could be thrown when the inserted element is copied. Because its type is unknown, we cannot know what exceptions are thrown.

Typically, an implementation of a virtual member function in a derived class can allow the member function to be called in more situations than are specified by the base class, so the precondition can be weaker in a derived class. The opposite, a stronger precondition, breaks substitutability.

A derived class implementation often does more than the postcondition of the base class promises because the implementation has an added state that is also modified. The opposite, a weaker postcondition, breaks substitutability.

Substitutability also requires that a derived class always fulfill the base class invariant. Otherwise, an object can be put in a state that the user of the class does not expect.

EXAMPLE 10.12   **Specification of an overriden member function**

A collection may be bounded or unbounded, so it is natural to specialize the base class `EmcCollection<T>`.

The class template, `EmcBoundedCollection`, represents a family of classes derived from an `EmcCollection` instantiation, which allows only a limited number of objects to be inserted. By preallocating storage, we can avoid a `bad_alloc` exception when an object is inserted. This is a stronger promise than is made by the base class, but that does not break substitutability because the precondition for `insert()` is the same.

```
virtual void insert(const T&);
// REQUIRE(! isFull())
// ENSURE(! isEmpty())
```

The class template, `EmcUnboundedCollection`, represents a family of classes derived from an `EmcCollection` instantiation, which allows any number of objects to be inserted. As long as the program does not run out of memory, objects can be inserted. We can no longer check in advance whether the insertion will succeed, so `! isFull()` is no longer a precondition; that is, the precondition is weaker.

```
virtual void insert(const T&);
// throw(bad_alloc)
// ENSURE(! isEmpty())
// ENSURE(OLD.size() + 1 == size())
```

On the other hand, a stronger postcondition has been added. An insertion must increase the size of the collection or throw a `bad_alloc` exception. The old postcondition that the collection is not empty after an insertion is a consequence of this new stronger postcondition because the size will always be larger than 0. It is mentioned here as a comment only.

Without this stronger postcondition, an implementation could simply overwrite stored objects instead of increasing the size of the collection. That is a behavior that the user probably does not expect when operating on an unbounded collection. A derived class should give additional constraints for how the base class interface is implemented.

```
// insertObject() works for any class with
// EmcUnboundedCollection<T> as a public base class.

template <class T>
void insertObject(EmcUnboundedCollection<T>& cref,
                  const T& element)  // throw (bad_alloc)
{
    // The precondition of
    // EmcUnboundedCollection<T>::insert is weaker than the
    // precondition for EmcCollection<T>::insert because an
    // unbounded collection is never full.

    cref.insert(element);
}
```

Rec. 10.9 Document the interface of template parameters.

A template defines a family of classes or functions. Apart from having template parameters that must be given values before it is used, a template is not very different from an ordinary class or function. Here we discuss what is different about templates: the presence of type parameters and the consequence of having classes and functions that are generated by the compiler. This discussion will help you both when you want to write your own templates and when you want to use existing templates.

Templates were originally introduced in C++ to make it possible to write type safe containers without having to use macros to change the stored type.

EXAMPLE 10.13   Describing template parameter requirements

EmcCollection is a class template whose instantiations are abstract classes.

```
// T must be: DefaultConstructible
//            CopyConstructible
//            Assignable
//            Destructible
//            EqualityComparable
```

```
template <class T>
class EmcCollection
{
   public:
      // ...
};
```

We have a comment to describe what is required for the type argument T in order to instantiate the template.

These requirements must be known to the user of the class. By having symbolic names for the most common requirements, we make the specification of template requirements shorter and easier to comprehend.

In the example above, we use names that are taken from the C++ standard library; they are defined as follows. If T is a type, the following expressions should be valid:

```
T t1;                // DefaultConstructible
T t2(t1);            // CopyConstructible
t2 = t1;             // Assignable
bool b = (t2 == t1); // EqualityComparable
// Destructible, an object on the stack can be created.
```

Sometimes we can also make more detailed assumptions, such as "T must have int T::hash() const."

The compiler checks that a template argument is suitable. For class templates, only the member function templates that are actually used will be instantiated. Some older compilers instantiate the whole class, but that is not standard behavior. A consequence is that a class template can be used with arguments that fulfill only a subset of the requirements, as long as member functions that require more are not used. This is not a recommended use of a class template because the user does not know how the requirements are related to individual member functions.

To make sure that the template arguments work properly, the class should have a private static member function that contains expressions that can be parsed only if the template arguments fulfill the complete set of requirements.

If this member function is instantiated, the full set of requirements will be checked by the compiler.

EXAMPLE 10.14 **Checking type constraints**

```
template <class T>
class EmcCollection
{
   public:
      // ...
      static void templateRequirements();
      // ...
};


template <class T>
void EmcCollection<T>::templateRequirements()
{
                           // T must be:
   T t1;                   // DefaultConstructible
   T t2(t1);               // CopyConstructible
   t2 = t1;                // Assignable
   bool b = (t2 == t1);    // EqualityComparable
}                          // Destructible
```

These checks do not help you to determine the performance characteristics of a type. If types with the wrong characteristics are used, the program may perform very poorly. If you document the time-complexity for different operations on the instantiation-bound types, the user will be able to avoid surprises.

A template instantiation could also have a set of types whose names ar qualified with template type parameters. These must also be taken in consideration when you specify templates.

EXAMPLE 10.15 **Performance characteristics of types**

A container in the standard library should provide the following two types:

value_type   Type of values stored by the container.

iterator   For access to objects in container.

The first type, value_type, is assumed to be costly to copy, because it should be possible to store any value in a container.

The second type, iterator, should behave as a pointer and is therefore assumed to be cheap to copy.

The consequence of this is that value_type objects are always passed as const references, whereas iterator objects are passed as values.

chapter eleven

Assertions

You probably write test programs to verify your implementation. To make sure that bugs are detected as early as possible, it is useful to check preconditions, postconditions and invariants inside your code. Many bugs originate from making the wrong assumption about what conditions should be true when writing the code. These checks should be done within the implementation of a class because you do not want to break encapsulation when testing the class. There is a performance cost to these checks. Normally you want to have checks that are easy to disable after testing is complete. This is easy to achieve using macros. This chapter is about the consequences of using assert macros.

RULES AND RECOMMENDATIONS

Rule 11.1   Do not let assertions change the state of the program.

Rec. 11.2   Remove all assertions from production code.

See Also

Rec. 10.7: If you use C++ to specify classes, assertions can be useful.

Rule 11.1 Do not let assertions change the state of the program.

Assertions are created as macros because they should be easy to remove from production code. You either use the assert macro in the standard library or create your own.

An assertion must not change the state of the program. If it does, the behavior of the program and the state of objects depend on whether the assertion is enabled. This makes it impossible to disable assertions after testing has been done.

EXAMPLE 11.1 **Standard assert macro**

```
#include <assert.h>

void check(int answer)
{
   assert(answer == 42);
   // ...
}
```

Rec. 11.2 Remove all assertions from production code.

All assertions should be removed from production code. If they are not, there is a chance that the behavior of the program will depend on them. The program will also run faster if unnecessary checks are removed.

Some conditions are not checked by assertions. You should not use assertions to check conditions that should always result in throwing an exception if the check fails. Such exceptions are part of the production code and should not be removable.

EXAMPLE 11.2 **Assertions and exceptions**

```
// Checked version

char& EmcString::at(size_t index) throw(EmcIndexOutOfRange)
{
   if (index >= lengthM)
   {
      throw EmcIndexOutOfRange(index);
   }

   return cpM[index];
}

// Unchecked version

char& EmcString::operator[](size_t index)
{
   assert(index < lengthM);
   return cpM[index];
}
```

chapter twelve

Error Handling

Errors can be reported and handled in a few different ways in a C++ program. Here, we concentrate on the use of exception handling, which has many advantages over the alternatives. By using exception handling, you can separate the error-handling code from the normal control flow and many different types of errors can be handled in one place. By allowing any amount of information to be passed with the exception, you have a better chance of making the correct decision when handling the error.

Different Ways to Report Errors

Runtime errors can be reported in a few different ways in a C++ program. Throwing exceptions or returning status codes from functions are two possibilities. It is important to always check error conditions, regardless of how they are reported.

RULES AND RECOMMENDATIONS

Rec. 12.1	Check for all errors reported from functions.
Rec. 12.2	Use exception handling instead of status values and error codes.

Rec. 12.1 Check for all errors reported from functions.

Rec. 12.2 Use exception handling instead of status values and error codes.

In C++, the best way to report an unexpected error condition is to throw an exception.

```
throw EmcException("Fatal error: Could not open file");
```

Throwing an exception is very similar to a `return` statement. When a function returns, local objects end their lifetimes and their destructors are called. The same thing happens when leaving a function by throwing an exception. A difference is that it is not obvious from reading the code which statement will throw an exception, but it is obvious where the function returns.

Throwing an exception is not the only way to report an error. Many programs reuse existing libraries written in C that report errors through status values and error codes instead of throwing exceptions.

A difference between these solutions is that it is not possible to ignore an exception. Unless there is a handler, or `catch` statement, that can handle the exception, the program will terminate. If that is not the desired result, the program must be modified.

It is important to handle exceptions, but it is even more important to always check status values returned from functions. If an error reported this way is ignored, there is no easy way of knowing what made the program crash. Such programs must also be modified, but it is much more difficult to know where.

EXAMPLE 12.1   **Checking status value**

The `socket()` function is a Unix library function that creates a communication channel between two processes. If the call succeeds, it returns a socket file descriptor that is `>= 0`; otherwise `-1` is returned.

```
// create socket
int socketfd = socket(AF_UNIX, SOCK_STREAM, 0);
if (socketfd < 0) // check status value
{
    // ...
}
```

The negative return value is a status value that tells the user that something did go wrong, but not the reason for failure. In this particular case, the global variable `errno` must be used to get a description of the error.

It seems natural to check status values returned from functions, but in reality there are huge amounts of code written that do not do these checks. The fact that status values can be ignored by the programmer is one of the reasons why exception handling in most cases is a better way of reporting errors.

Using status values works well only if all functions along a call chain are given the chance to handle the error. This requires the programmer to mix code that represents the ordinary flow of control with code that is run only when an error is reported.

With exception handling it is possible to separate code that handles errors from the ordinary flow of control. Less code needs to be written because exception handling can be localized to one function along a call chain. It is also possible to handle many different exceptions with the same piece of code by specifying a handler for an exception base class, or with an ellipsis (. . .).

```
try
{   // ordinary flow of control
    f();
    g();
}
catch(...)      // handler for any kind of exception
{
    // error handling
}
```

An additional difficulty with status values is that constructors and some overloaded operators cannot return values, which means that a status value must either be passed as a reference argument or be stored by the object.

If you use exception handling instead of status values, the functions will need fewer arguments and return values, which makes them much easier to use. Another advantage is that if you do not have any way of recovering from an error reported as an exception, you can simply ignore it and it will be propagated up along the call chain.

An additional benefit is that because an exception is an object, an arbitrary amount of error information can be stored in an exception object. The more information that is available, the greater the chance that the correct decision is made for how to handle the error.

EXAMPLE 12.2 Throwing an exception

If we use functions that return status values, it is possible to provide a wrapper function that throws an exception instead of
returning a status value. By doing so, we only need to check the
status value in one place.

```
class EmcException
{
   public:
      // ...
      // EmcException objects can be printed
      friend ostream&
         operator<<(ostream&, const EmcException&);
      // ...
};

class EmcSystemException : public EmcException
{
   public:
      EmcSystemException(const char* message);
      // ...
};

int emcSocket(int family, int type, int protocol)
throw(EmcSystemException)
{
   // create socket
   int socketfd = socket(family, type, protocol);
   if (socketfd < 0)// check status value
   {
      throw EmcSystemException("Socket");
   }
   return socketfd;
}
```

An even better solution is to encapsulate the calls inside a class.
Thus, errors reported by functions such as socket() can be
translated into exceptions that are more meaningful to the user,
and can also encapsulate all reasons why a particular member
function failed. This also allows the user to modify the implementation and to replace sockets with any other mechanism for inter-
process communication, without revealing such changes to the
user. We have not done that because we wanted to keep the example simple.

When to Throw Exceptions

A programmer can throw an exception anytime, so rules are needed to govern when exceptions are thrown so that both the user and the supplier of class libraries can write code that is robust and correct.

RULES AND RECOMMENDATIONS

Rec. 12.3   **Throw exceptions only when a function fails to do what it is expected to do.**

Rec. 12.4   **Do not throw exceptions as a way of reporting uncommon values from a function.**

Rule 12.5   **Do not let destructors called during stack unwinding throw exceptions.**

Rec. 12.6   **Constructors of types thrown as exceptions should not themselves throw exceptions.**

See Also

Rec. 10.6: How to describe what a function is expected to do.

Rule 12.8: Classes that must have a destructor.

Rec. 12.3 Throw exceptions only when a function fails to do what it is expected to do.

When should an exception be thrown? It is possible to throw exceptions whenever a function encounters an unusual case, but we do not recommend that because too frequent use of exceptions makes the control flow difficult to follow.

It is appropriate to use exceptions as a way to report unexpected errors. What is unexpected depends on the class specification and when the error is detected. The user and the implementor often have different views of what is unexpected. If preconditions and postconditions are used to specify behavior of member functions, it is possible to be more precise.

- A precondition violation is an unexpected error for the implementor, but not for the user.
- A postcondition violation is an unexpected error for the user, but not for the implementor, if we assume the precondition was valid on entry into the function.

We think that an exception should be thrown only to report an unexpected error to the user. We must give the user a chance to handle an error that could not have been prevented by a precondition check.

Such exceptions are part of the class interface and tell the user in what way the function could not fulfill its obligation to make the postcondition valid. Exceptions thrown for any other reason than this are questionable, but not completely forbidden.

If you do not follow this recommendation, exceptions may be thrown even when the user could have prevented them from being thrown. A precondition violation is a good example.

Because it is the user's obligation to make the precondition valid, such errors are only found in incorrect programs. What is the best way to handle such errors: To recover from the error and to let the program continue, or rewrite the program? We prefer the second alternative and recommend you to check preconditions only as a way to find bugs in your program.

It is useful to check the precondition because that prevents the user from writing incorrect code, but if we assume that incorrectly written programs should be corrected, how to report precondition errors is less important. Whether an exception should be thrown or the program should terminate by calling `abort()` is a matter of taste and depends on the situation. Exception handling allows the program to terminate in a more controlled manner.

EXAMPLE 12.3   **Member function with a precondition**

When an `EmcString` object is initialized with a `char` array, a precondition is that a non-null pointer must be passed as argument.

The implementation does not throw an exception because the user can prevent a null pointer from being passed as parameter. Here, it is the user's obligation to make sure that the member function can do what it is expected to do.

An `EmcString` object stores a pointer to a `char` array that is allocated with `new`. The user cannot possibly determine beforehand that `new` might fail to allocate the necessary memory needed for the allocation, so the implementation must report the error by throwing an exception.

```
EmcString::EmcString(const char* cp) throw(bad_alloc)
: lengthM(strlen(cp))
{
    // PRECONDITION: cp != 0
```

```
    // operator new() will throw bad_alloc
    // if allocation fails
    cpM = new char[lengthM + 1];
    strcpy(cpM, cp);
}
```

Rec. 12.4 Do not throw exceptions as a way of reporting uncommon values from a function.

A consequence of the recommendation that exceptions should be thrown only if a function fails to do what it is expected to is that exceptions should not be used as a way of reporting uncommon values from a function.

It is important to remember why exceptions are a bad choice in these situations. If an exception is thrown, that exception must be handled, or the control flow of the program will change in a way that cannot be predicted. Throwing an exception for the sole purpose of changing the control flow is therefore not recommended.

Your code can be difficult to understand if you throw exceptions in many different situations, ranging from a way to report unusual threads in your code to reporting fatal runtime problems. Exception handling is also often a much less efficient way to change the control flow in a program than passing along error codes.

EXAMPLE 12.4   Returning a special value to report a failure

The `find()` function in the standard library is a good example of a function that could fail, but for which throwing an exception is inappropriate.

The standard library uses iterators to traverse through collections of objects. The iterators are modeled after pointers, and ordinary pointers are therefore a special type of iterator.

An input iterator is a special kind of iterator that allows you to read one element at a time in a forward direction only. If such an object is assigned to an element in a collection, after being incremented a number of times, it will eventually be equal to the iterator pointing at the last element in the collection.

```
template<class InputIterator, class T>
InputIterator
find(InputIterator first, InputIterator last,
    const T& value);
```

The function `find()` is defined to return the first iterator between the first and last elements (but not counting last itself) that points to a `T` equal to `value`. If no such value is found, it will return the last iterator. It is quite common not to find what you are looking for, so it is not reasonable to call it a programming failure if that happens. Therefore, `find()` is defined to return `last` if `value` was not found in the sequence.

Rule 12.5 Do not let destructors called during stack unwinding throw exceptions.

There are a few places where exceptions should not be used to report errors. Inside destructors is one such place.

A `try` block defines both a scope and a set of exception handlers. Before continuing the execution inside a handler, the program will leave the scope of the `try` block. This means that destructors for local variables inside the `try` block must be run to properly end their lifetimes.

If an exception is thrown during this process and not handled by the destructor, the library function `terminate()` is called. This function terminates the program. If that happens, there is a good chance that some external resources managed by local objects have not been released, which could mean that the program cannot be restarted unless the user manually releases such resources.

There are two ways to avoid this: Either you make sure not to call code that might throw exceptions inside destructors or you catch all exceptions thrown in destructors. The second alternative requires some additional programming because you must add a `try` block with exception handlers to the implementation of the destructor.

A problem is that you may want to allow the user to handle exceptions thrown under normal circumstances. A recent addition to C++ is the function `uncaught_exception()`, which reports `true` if exceptions are handled and `false` if they are not. If your compiler supports this function, then you can check whether it is OK to rethrow the exception. If it is not supported, you should ignore all exceptions thrown inside the destructor.

EXAMPLE 12.5   **Preventing exceptions inside destructors**

Logging is useful if you want to know what made a program crash. However, it can slow down a program because output must be written to a file or the console. One way to improve performance is to cache the log messages in memory and write them to a file only when something unexpected happens, such as when an exception is thrown.

The class `EmcLog` is used to implement such a scheme. The class stores the log messages and writes them to a log file after a call to the member function `flush()`. The idea is to allocate objects of this class on the stack and to use the function `uncaught_ exception()` inside the destructor to check whether an exception has been thrown. If an exception has been thrown, we append to the log file.

```cpp
class EmcLog
{
   public:

      class CouldNotOpenFile : public EmcException
      {
         public:
            CouldNotOpenFile(const EmcString& fileName);
         private:
            EmcString fileNameM;
      };

      EmcLog(const EmcString& fileName);
      ~EmcLog();

      void message(const EmcString&); // store log message
      void flush(); throw(CouldNotOpenFile);
                                      // append to log file

      // ...

   private:
      EmcLog(const EmcLog&);                // Non-copyable
      EmcLog& operator=(const EmcLog&);

      EmcQueue<EmcString> messageCacheM; // log messages
      EmcString           filenameM;     // log file
};

EmcLog::~EmcLog()
{
   if (uncaught_exception())
   {
      flush();
   }
}
```

We must also call `uncaught_exception()` inside `flush()` because this function throws an exception if it is unable to open the log file. Because an exception must not propagate from the destructor, such an error must be ignored when `flush()` is called by the destructor.

```
void EmcLog::flush() throw (CouldNotOpenFile)
{
    ofstream out(filenameM, ios::app);
    if (!out && !uncaught_exception())
    {
        throw CouldNotOpenFile (EmcString(fileNameM));
    }
    // write messages to log
    // ...
}
```

Rec. 12.6 Constructors of types thrown as exceptions should not themselves throw exceptions.

Another place where exceptions should be prevented from slipping out is inside the constructors of objects thrown as exceptions.

The problem here is that if the constructor throws an exception, the user gets the wrong exception to catch. The user may catch the exception, and even try to recover from the problem, but the user is actually trying to handle another error. The real problem is lost and forgotten.

For copy constructors, there is another problem. The exception object is copied to an area managed by the exception-handling system before leaving the scope in which the throw is done. If this copy fails, `terminate()` is called.

EXAMPLE 12.6   Exception class constructor

The exception class `EmcException` has a constructor with a `const char*` parameter. It seems natural to have a string data member to store that value. Most string classes allocate memory with the `new` operator. This means that if the class has such a data member, the constructor of this class will throw the standard exception `bad_alloc` if memory allocation fails.

A way to avoid that would be to limit the size of the string. Such a solution has the advantage of being exception safe, but you have to make sure that the allocated string is big enough.

```
class EmcException
{
   public:
      EmcException(const char* message);
      // ...

   private:
      enum { maxSizeM = 100 };

      int    lengthM;
      char   messageM[maxSizeM+1];
};

EmcException::EmcException(const char* message)
{
   size_t actualLength = strlen(message);
   lengthM = min(maxSizeM,actualLength);
   strncpy(messageM, message, lengthM);
   messageM[lengthM] = '\0';
}
```

Exception Safe Code

It is necessary to prevent memory leaks and other errors that are related to how resources are acquired and released. By managing all resources with objects, you will find it less difficult to write code that properly manages resources.

RULES AND RECOMMENDATIONS

Rec. 12.7   Use objects to manage resources.

Rule 12.8   A resource managed by an object must be released by the object's destructor.

Rec. 12.9   Use stack objects instead of free store objects.

Rec. 12.10   Before letting any exceptions propagate out of a member function, make certain that the class invariant holds and, if possible, leave the state of the object unchanged.

See Also   Rec. 5.11: When to implement copy constructor, copy assignment operator, and destructor.

Rec. 10.6: Definition of class invariant.

Rec. 12.7 Use objects
to manage resources.

A resource is something that more than one program needs, but for which availability is limited. Good examples are memory and other operating system resources such as sockets, file descriptors, drawing contexts, shared memory, and database locks. The most important to manage are those that are not released when the program terminates.

It is essential to correctly acquire and release resources. Unless you acquire a resource for the whole lifetime of the program, the resource should be acquired and released within a block of code. It is common to have a function that is called at the beginning of the block and another function that is called at the end of the block.

1. Call function to acquire resource.
2. Use the resource.
3. Call function to release resource.

The question is how to make sure that the statements for both acquiring and releasing the resource are run. The problem is that the control flow of a C++ program is not sequential because a function could return either the normal way or by throwing an exception.

A fundamental idea behind C++ exception handling is that resources should be allocated in the constructor and deallocated in the destructor of a class. Resource acquisition is initialization, in other words, resources should be managed by objects.

It is convenient to use the constructor and the destructor for this purpose because they are automatically called when the objects start and end their lifetimes. No additional function calls are needed to properly manage the resource. This is also the best way because destructors are the only member functions that are called before leaving a scope after an exception has been thrown.

If your code is a combination of application logic and error-handling code, this is probably because it does not have exception safe classes. You should always try to separate error-handling code from the application control flow.

Rule 12.8 A resource
managed by an object
must be released by the
object's destructor.

You should always release a resource in the destructor. If any other member functions must be called, you might have to catch the exception and propagate it a number of times before handling it. This is a much more complex solution because additional code must be written.

Rec. 12.9 Use stack objects instead of free store objects.

You should also allocate objects carefully. C++ has objects with static, automatic, and dynamic storage duration. Objects created with new are most expensive to allocate and most difficult to use. Whenever possible, you should create an object on the stack instead of with new. Stack objects are less expensive to allocate and there is no risk of memory leaks as long as you use only exception safe classes.

You should create an object with new only if the lifetime is not controlled by you, not just because you need a pointer to the object.

Exception handling has made it even more difficult to manage free store objects. Each free store object must always be accessible through either a static pointer or an object on the stack that owns the object.

It is dangerous and inconvenient to have only local pointers to objects allocated with new. If a local pointer is the only way to access an object created with new, your code will have a memory leak, unless you have a try block that catches all possible exceptions.

EXAMPLE 12.7   **Unsafe memory allocation**

The most fundamental resource to manage in C++ programs is dynamically allocated memory. The most obvious example is a string class; examples of how to write such a class are shown in Chapters 5 and 7.

The following code is unsafe because it contains a memory leak. The problem is that the delete statement is not reached if an exception is thrown within the function.

```
void f()                    // Not recommended
{
   int* ip = new int(1); // create int with new
   g(*ip);
   // memory leak if g() throws exception
   delete ip;             // not reached
}

void g(int i)
{
   throw i;               // Not recommended to throw int
}
```

EXAMPLE 12.8   **Having a `try` block to manage memory**

It is possible to rewrite our previous example so that the memory leak is avoided without introducing any new classes. The function should have a `try` block with a handler that catches all possible exceptions.

```
void f()                    // Not recommended
{
   int* ip = new int(1);  // create int with new
   try
   {
      g(*ip);
      // memory safe even if g() throws exception
      delete ip;          // not reached
   }
   catch(...)              // catch any exception
   {
      delete ip;
      throw;              // Rethrowing the exception
   }
}
```

EXAMPLE 12.9   **Exception safe allocation of free store objects**

The best way to manage objects allocated with `new` is to have a local object that manages the memory instead of a pointer and a delete statement. You code will be shorter and less difficult to write.

We recommend that you use the class template `auto_ptr`, supplied with the C++ standard library.

```
void f()
{
   auto_ptr<int> ip(new int(1)); // create int with new
   g(*ip);
   // memory safe even if g() throws exception
}
```

If you want to keep control of the deletion of the object managed by `auto_ptr`, you must explicitly call `release()` to tell `auto_ptr` to give up ownership of the object. If you do not do that, `auto_ptr` will delete the object when its destructor is run.

Rec. 12.10 Before letting any exceptions propagate out of a member function, make certain that the class invariant holds and, if possible, leave the state of the object unchanged.

Throwing an exception should not damage the state of your objects. If possible, preserve the state of the current object before leaving the scope of a member function by throwing an exception. If that is not possible, try to restore the state so that the object's destructor is safe to call. By doing that, you increase the chance that the program can recover from the exception because if the current object is a local object, its destructor will be called. As we said before, such a destructor must not throw exceptions or fail in any other way.

Here we discuss state only after the object has been initialized. When exceptions are thrown by constructors, destructors are called only for member objects that are completely initialized. Only these, not the complete object, must be in valid states if an exception is thrown inside the constructor.

All constructors should leave the object in a valid state so that its destructor can be called without any errors. That guarantees successful cleanup of member objects when they leave the scope of the constructor.

When designing classes you should try to figure out which operations could throw exceptions, then minimize the amount of time that the object is in an invalid state. If possible, modify the state of the object only after all dangerous functions has been called. If that is not possible, either make it possible to restore the state of the object or give the object a default value before throwing the exception.

When writing templates you must decide what operations are allowed to throw exceptions. If you do not make any such decisions, an exception could be thrown when the state of the object is invalid.

If possible, whenever a member function modifies the state of an object, avoid changing the state of the actual object and instead modify a copy of the state. If we can switch the state of the object without getting any exceptions, a template can allow any exceptions to be thrown when updating the copy, not the original, thereby keeping the state of the original object unchanged.

Better performance can be achieved by making stronger assumptions about what exceptions can be thrown, but then the class is less reusable. As always, there is a tradeoff between flexibility and performance.

EXAMPLE 12.10   Exception safe copy assignment operator

The template `EmcStack` uses a built-in array, `vectorM`, to store copies of objects. The pointer `topM` stores an index to the next element in the array to assign. The data member `allocatedM` stores the number of currently allocated objects, and is always a positive number.

```
template<class T>
class EmcStack
{
   public:
      enum       { defaultSizeM = 100 };

      EmcStack(int size = defaultSizeM);
      EmcStack(const EmcStack& s);
      ~EmcStack();
      EmcStack& operator=(const EmcStack& s);
      // ...
      bool      empty() const;
      const T&  top() const;
      void      push(const T& i);
      T         pop();

   private:
      unsigned  allocatedM;
      T*        vectorM;
      int       topM;
};
```

We want to provide an exception safe implementation of the copy assignment operator for `EmcStack`. Our strategy is to make all dangerous operations before modifying the state of the object, so that the state is valid even if an exception is thrown.

In order to avoid memory leaks, we also use an object of the class `EmcAutoArrayPtr<T>` to manage memory. `EmcAutoArrayPtr` is a template that is similar to the class `auto_ptr` in the standard library, but manages arrays of objects instead of individual objects.

```
template<class T>
EmcStack<T>& EmcStack<T>::operator=(const EmcStack<T>& s)
{
   if (this != &s)
   {
      // operator new may throw bad_alloc
      EmcAutoArrayPtr<T> newVector(new T[s.allocatedM]);

      // copy elements
      for (int i = 0; i < s.topM; i++)
      {
         newVector[i] = s.vectorM[i];
      }
      delete [] vectorM;

      // assign to object
      topM      = s.topM;
      vectorM   = newVector.release();
      allocatedM = s.allocatedM;
   }
   return *this;
}
```

If memory allocation were costly, we could have tried to optimize memory by copying to existing storage already used by the object, as was done in Example 5.12. However, such an implementation would be much more difficult to make exception safe. If an exception is thrown when assigning to an element of the object's representation, the state of the object will be undefined and probably corrupt.

Exception Types

Exception handling makes it possible to localize error handling to fewer places in the code. The number of try blocks should not have to grow exponentially with the size of the program. Exception classes should be organized in hierarchies to minimize the number of exception handlers.

Exception hierarchies allow for object-oriented error handling; that is, you can use dynamic binding when handling errors. This means that the same handler can be used for different types of exceptions. This makes the code more readable and easier to maintain.

Rec. 12.11	Throw only objects of class type.
Rec. 12.12	Group related exception types by using inheritance.
Rec. 12.13	Catch objects only by reference.

See Also   Rule 7.6: Why objects are passed by reference.

Rule 10.8: Behavior of derived classes.

Rec. 12.11 Throw only
objects of class type.

An object can be thrown if it can be copied and destroyed. This makes it possible to throw values of built-in types, pointers, arrays, or objects. You should throw only objects of class type; otherwise it will not be possible to distinguish errors by the type, only by the value. There is nothing in the language to prevent a value from representing many things, but a type name must be unique within a program.

If we throw a general-purpose type, such as an `int`, the value must represent exactly one type of error, or there is a risk that the wrong error might be handled. We must use a value that is globally unique, a solution that makes it difficult to add new classes or to use new class libraries.

The exception type should always represent the type of error, and it should be a class that is used for exception handling only.

An additional benefit of throwing objects is that they can contain any amount of data. You can have a data member that stores a description of the error, and you can print that description inside the handler.

EXAMPLE 12.11   **Throwing an object of built-in type**

The `socket()` function has many reasons for failure, each of them represented as an integer value. For example, `EACESS` is returned if the function is denied permission to create the socket, and `ENOMEM` is returned if there is no available memory.

Suppose you would like to translate these error codes into exceptions. It is possible, but not recommended, to throw an `int` containing the error value. The problem with this approach is that you cannot catch different objects (in this case different integers), only different types. With an integer approach such as this you would be forced to have one single `catch` clause with a big `switch` statement to indicate how, or whether, an error should be handled, depending on the integer value. Furthermore, this solution works only if you know where the exception originates. Nothing prevents two functions from throwing the same value to represent two different errors.

Rec. 12.12 Group related exception types by using inheritance.

A `try` block could have as many handlers as there are exception types, but it is good to limit the number of handlers.

You can group related exception types by using inheritance. This is necessary when you want to handle many different types of exceptions the same way.

Rec. 12.13 Catch objects only by reference.

It is a good idea to catch a reference to a base class so that the user can ignore the exact type of the exception that was thrown.

It is important to note here that it is possible to derive new classes without affecting the user's code. The handler for the base class will handle exceptions of derived classes. Instead of having many handlers for each derived class, you can have a handler for a base class. In the `catch` clause we are supposed to try to handle an error, so it makes sense to group exception classes in hierarchies according to how they can be handled.

Another reason why exceptions should be caught by reference is that you can lose information when a derived class object is copied to a base class object instead of being passed by reference. Only the base class part will be copied; the derived class part is sliced off. The same thing could happen when passing objects by value to a function.

It can be useful to have nested exception classes. If you derive from that class and from a general purpose exception class, you can organize your handlers based not only on error type, but also on where the exception was thrown. Inheritance is used to control type matching rather than to create special versions of the base class.

EXAMPLE 12.12   Inheritance of exception classes

It is good to have a general exception class at the top that allows you to print a description of the error. Most users are satisfied with knowing what went wrong and would have only one handler for a whole hierarchy of exception classes.

In our examples we use the class `EmcException`, which stores strings that describe the error condition.

```
class EmcException
{
    public:
        EmcException(const char* message);

        // EmcException objects can be printed
        friend ostream&
            operator<<(ostream&, const EmcException&);

    protected:
        // hook for derived classes
        virtual ostream& printOn(ostream& o) const;

    private:
        enum { maxSizeM = 100 };

        int  lengthM;
        char messageM[maxSizeM+1];
};
```

The class provides a virtual member function `printOn()`, which can be overridden by derived classes.

```
ostream& EmcException::printOn(ostream& o) const
{
    o << messageM;
    return o;
}

ostream& operator<<(ostream& o, const EmcException& e)
{
    return e.printOn(o);
}
```

If an object of the class `EmcException` or any class derived from it is handled, the message printed depends on both the type of the exception and the message stored by the object.

We have also used the class `EmcSystemException`, which is derived from `EmcException`.

```
class EmcSystemException : public EmcException
{
   public:
      EmcSystemException(const char* cp);
      // ...
   protected:
      virtual ostream& printOn(ostream& o) const;
   private:
      static const char* const headerM;
};
```

It overrides printOn() so that a header is provided for each error message. The global variable errno is used as an index in the table of error messages for the Unix system calls, sys_errlist.

```
const char* const
   EmcSystemException::headerM = "System call failed: ";

extern char* sys_errlist[]; // Table with error messages
                            // for UNIX system calls

ostream& EmcSystemException::printOn(ostream& o) const
{
   o << headerM << sys_errlist[::errno] << ": ";
   return EmcException::printOn(o);
}
```

EXAMPLE 12.13   Handling many exceptions with one handler

A handler for EmcException can be used to handle an EmcSystemException because the latter class inherits from EmcException.

```
try
{  // ordinary flow of control
   int socketfd = emcSocket(AF_UNIX, SOCK_STREAM, 0);
   // ...
}
catch(EmcException& e) // handler for any exception class
                       // derived from EmcException
{
   cerr << e << endl;
   exit(1);
}
```

Error Recovery

Sometimes exceptions of unknown types may propagate through your code. It is important to know which of these you should catch and which ones you should let the user handle.

RULES AND RECOMMENDATIONS

Rule 12.14   **Always catch exceptions the user is not supposed to know about.**

Rec. 12.15   **Do not catch exceptions you are not supposed to know about.**

See Also   Rec. 10.6, Rec. 12.16: Specifying exceptions for a class.

Rule 12.14 Always catch exceptions the user is not supposed to know about.

Hidden implementation details are an important property of well-written programs because they enable you to make changes without affecting the user.

Imagine a hierarchy of libraries where some libraries are implemented on top of other libraries. To be able to change or replace lower-level classes without affecting the user, you must catch all exceptions that the user is not supposed to know about. Otherwise, an exception of a class unknown to the user could terminate the program or be caught by a handler with a . . . parameter list. In either case, the user does not know what caused the exception to be thrown. All exceptions that reach the user should be known to the user so that he or she can determine why the exception was thrown and how to prevent it from being thrown. You should try to avoid writing programs that simply crash without indicating what went wrong.

Rec. 12.15 Do not catch exceptions you are not supposed to know about.

On the other hand, there are exceptions that may propagate through your code that you should not catch or translate. The most obvious example is exceptions that might be thrown from template parameters.

The template designer must specify under what circumstances a variable of a type given as template parameter is allowed to throw exceptions. It is very difficult, if not impossible, to write templates that can be instantiated with a type that throws exceptions in places that are not known in advance. These exceptions should usually be propagated to the user of the template because only the user knows what exceptions to expect.

There are other cases where you may use code that can throw unknown exceptions. For example, the user might supply a pointer to a sorting or hash function, which you will use inside your code. In such cases you should let the supplier of the function take care of all the exceptions that are thrown.

Exception Specifications

Exception specifications are used to document what exceptions are thrown from a function. We recommend that you use them as much as possible.

RULES AND RECOMMENDATIONS

Rec. 12.16 Use exception specifications to declare which exceptions might be thrown from a function.

See Also Rec. 12.3: When to throw exceptions.

Rec. 12.16 Use exception specifications to declare which exceptions might be thrown from a function.

Exceptions are part of the class interface and must be handled by the user when they are thrown. The language gives you an option to declare the exceptions thrown by a function. If a function does not have an exception specification, that function is allowed to throw any type of exception.

We recommend that you use exception specifications as much as possible. Because they are part of the language, the compiler will check that the exception classes exist and are available to the user.

It is a program bug if a function with an exception specification throws an exception that has not been specified. If that happens, the default is to either terminate the program or, if the exception specification includes bad_exception, to throw an object of that class instead. You should avoid this situation if you can.

A consequence of the fact that template functions should propagate exceptions is that a template function should only rarely have an exception specification. It should have one only when the exact set of exception types that can be thrown are known in advance. A template function should probably not have an exception specification if the type of the exception thrown depends on a type argument.

EXAMPLE 12.14   **Exception specification**

```
char& EmcString::at(size_t index) throw(EmcIndexOutOfRange)
{
    if (index > lengthM)
    {
        throw EmcIndexOutOfRange(index);
    }
    return cpM[index]
}
```

chapter thirteen

Parts of C++ to Avoid

There are parts of C++ that should be avoided. C++ comes with many new standard library classes and templates that in many cases replace functions inherited from the C standard library. Also, certain parts of the language that are inherited from C are no longer needed; either better language constructs exist or there are classes or templates to use instead.

Library Functions to Avoid

C++ has inherited all parts of the library defined by the C standard. Some of the functions provided by the C standard library are not well-suited for C++ programming and should not be used.

RULES AND RECOMMENDATIONS

Rec. 13.1	Use `new` and `delete` instead of `malloc`, `calloc`, `realloc`, and `free`.
Rule 13.2	Use the `iostream` library instead of C-style I/O.
Rule 13.3	Do not use `setjmp()` and `longjmp()`.

149

Rec. 13.4   Use overloaded functions and chained function calls instead of functions with an unspecified number of arguments.

See Also   Rec. 7.15, Rule 7.16: How to overload functions and operators.

Rule 8.1–Rule 8.2: How to use `new` and `delete`.

Rec. 12.2: Exception handling can be used instead of `setjmp` and `longjmp`.

Rec. 13.1 Use `new` and `delete` instead of `malloc`, `calloc`, `realloc`, and `free`.

You should avoid all memory-handling functions from the standard C-library (such as `malloc`, `calloc`, `realloc`, and `free`) because they do not call constructors for new objects or destructors for deleted objects.

It is also dangerous to mix C and C++ allocation of memory, such as

- Calling `delete` for a pointer obtained via `malloc`
- Calling `malloc` for objects having constructors
- Calling `free` for anything allocated using `new`
- Calling `realloc` for anything allocated using `new`

Complete avoidance of C memory handling is therefore recommended.

Rule 13.2 Use the `iostream` library instead of C-style I/O.

For similar reasons the `iostream` library is better to use than the `stdio` library. Functions in the `stdio` library cannot be used for user-defined objects.

EXAMPLE 13.1   **C-style I/O is not adequate for objects**

```
EmcString s;
cin >> s;                    // Yes: this works

scanf("%??", s);             // NO: this does not work
```

It is not possible to extend the set of formats understood by `scanf`.

If optimal efficiency is required, the `stdio` library is sometimes better than the `iostream` library. This is not a universal truth, however, so you should do performance benchmarks before you start to use the `stdio` library. If you use it, localize the code so that it is easy to replace.

Rule 13.3 Do not use setjmp() and longjmp().

The normal way to leave a function is by using a return statement that gives control back to the calling function. If a serious error has been encountered, this can be an unwise thing to do: The calling function could recover from the failure, and when the program crashes it is difficult to find out what went wrong. The correct thing to do in C++ is to throw an exception. The library functions setjmp() and longjmp() can be used to simulate exception handling. Unfortunately, the behavior of these functions is very platform-dependent. Even worse is the fact that destructors are not called for bypassed objects when longjmp() is called. You should therefore avoid them altogether.

Rec. 13.4 Use overloaded functions and chained function calls instead of functions with an unspecified number of arguments.

Functions with an unspecified number of arguments should be avoided because they are a common cause of bugs that are hard to find. For example, the compiler is not able to check that an argument is of the type expected by the function. Such checks must instead be done by the function in runtime.

In most cases in C++ it is possible to use overloaded functions or operators instead, and to chain the function calls by returning references to operate on. Such solutions are more type-safe.

EXAMPLE 13.2   **Passing objects to** printf()

The function printf() should not be given an object as argument even if the object is of a class that can be implicitly converted to a type that printf() knows how to handle.

```
class DangerousString
{
   public:
      DangerousString(const char* cp);
      operator const char*() const; // Conversion operator
      // ...
};

DangerousString hello = "Hello World!";
cout << hello << endl;              // Works perfectly
printf("%s\n", hello);             // Garbage is printed
```

In this case operator const char*() is called when the string is passed to cout, but this does not happen for the string when it is passed to printf(). When a string object is passed as argument to printf(), no implicit conversion takes place and the bit pattern for the object is printed as a string.

EXAMPLE 13.3   **Overloading of** `operator<<`

```
class EmcString
{
  public:
    EmcString(const char* cp);
    // ...
};

ostream& operator<<(ostream& os, const EmcString& s);

EmcString s = "Hello World!";
cout << s << endl;            // uses overloaded operator
```

Language Constructs to Avoid

A few parts of the C++ language should be avoided because they are too error prone to be worth using.

RULES AND RECOMMENDATIONS

Rule 13.5   **Do not use macros instead of constants, enums, functions, or type definitions.**

Rec. 13.6   **Use an array class instead of built-in arrays.**

Rec. 13.7   **Do not use unions.**

See Also   Rule 2.3: Macros should be used in include guards.

Rec. 10.3: Polymorphism and inheritance can often replace selection statements and unions.

Rec. 15.13: Macros can be used for writing forward-compatible code.

Style A.6–Style A.7: How include guards are written.

Rule 13.5 Do not use macros instead of constants, enums, functions, or type definitions.

In C, macros are often used for defining constants. In C++, a better alternative is to use `enum` values or `const` declared variables. Macros do not obey the normal scope rules for the language, and this is a common source of errors. The compiler can seldom give meaningful error messages if the error is caused by a macro replacement.

EXAMPLE 13.4   **Macros do not obey scope rules**

```
#define SIZE 1024              // Not recommended
const size_t SIZE = 1024;      // Compilation error
```

Macro names should be all uppercase letters to help avoid unexpected macro replacements by the preprocessor. This is one reason why you should not have normal identifiers in all uppercase letters.

Constants defined by the language obey the scope rules of the language and can be enclosed inside a class.

EXAMPLE 13.5   **Recommended way to define constants**

You can often define constants within a class.

```
class X
{
    public:
        // ...
    private:
        static const size_t maxBuf = 1024;
        enum Color {green, yellow, red};
};

// Definition of static const member
const size_t X::maxBuf;
```

EXAMPLE 13.6   **Using an** enum **instead of** static const int

Older compilers do not allow you to define ordinary constants inside a class. A common trick is to use an anonymous enum instead.

```
class X
{
        // ...
    private:
        enum { maxBuf = 1024 };
        enum Color {green, yellow, red};
};
```

Another advantage of using constants instead of macros is that many debuggers see the code only as it looks after preprocessing. Inside a debugger it is possible to print the value of a constant, but not a macro value. Therefore, constants make it easier to debug a program.

Macros are often used in C as a way to avoid the function-call overhead for time-critical functions.

EXAMPLE 13.7   **Function-like macro,** SQUARE

```
// Not recommended to have function-like macro
#define SQUARE(x) x*x
```

There are many problems with function-like macros. Because the arguments are pure textual replacements, the consequences of using complex expressions as arguments are often surprising.

```
int i = SQUARE(3 + 4);
// Wrong result: i = (3 + 4 * 3 + 4) == 19, not 49
```

It is common to add parentheses to the definition to avoid some bugs.

```
// Parentheses to avoid precedence bugs
#define SQUARE(x) ((x)*(x))
```

But there are some bugs for which there is no good solution. If an argument is used more than once and an expression is passed as argument, the expression will be evaluated more than once.

```
int a = 2; int b = SQUARE(a++);
// Unknown result: b = 4 or 6 depending on when the value
// of postfix ++ is evaluated.
```

Inline functions in C++ are often a better choice because they allow you to avoid the function call overhead and still have something that behaves as a function.

EXAMPLE 13.8   **Inline function,** square

```
inline int square(int x) // Recommended
{
   return x * x;
};

int c = 2;
int d = square(c++);      // d = (2 * 2) == 4
```

Another advantage of inline functions compared to macros is that they are type-safe, which means that the compiler will give meaningful error messages when a function is used with the wrong type of arguments.

EXAMPLE 13.9   **Function-like macros are not type-safe**

```
int i = SQUARE("hello");    // Error: Illegal operands
```

Macros are also sometimes used to introduce synonyms for a type. A better solution is to use a `typedef`.

EXAMPLE 13.10   **How to define synonyms for a type**

```
#define Velocity int        // Not recommended
typedef int Velocity;       // Recommended
```

Macros should be used only as include guards and for very special purposes such as forward-compatibility macro packages (exceptions, templates, and runtime type identification).

Rec. 13.6 Use an array class instead of built-in arrays.

There are many potential bugs involved in using pointers to access built-in arrays. For example, when traversing an array, it is common to access too few or too many elements. Memory management can also be a big problem. It is almost always better to use an array template instead, and fortunately the standard library for C++ provides such a class.

There are a few other problems with the built-in arrays. They are of a fixed size, which means that the whole array must be copied if you need to increase its size. If the size changes often this can be bad for the performance of the program. In most cases it is better to use a class that handles growth in an efficient way.

Another problem is that there is no bounds checking, which means that you can access a memory area outside the array if you are not careful.

When accessing an array, the index is used simply to find the address of an element in the array. An array is treated as a pointer to the first element and the index is the offset to the element.

The fact that an array is treated as a pointer when passed to functions is a common source of errors. It is especially dangerous to have arrays of objects. Because the size of derived class objects in most cases is different from the size of base class objects, the offset between elements in an array of base class objects is different from the offset between elements in an array of derived class objects. C++ allows a derived class pointer to be assigned to a base class pointer, with the consequence that a compiler cannot prevent you from passing an array of derived class objects to a function that expects a pointer to an array of base class objects. When accessing elements in the array, you will get pointers within objects rather than pointers to objects. This is yet another reason to avoid the built-in arrays.

EXAMPLE 13.11   **Passing an array to a function**

```
// Fruit is a base class

void printFruits(Fruit* fruits, size_t size)
// Not recommended to pass arrays to functions
{
    for (size_t i = 0; i < size; i++)
    {
        cout << fruits[i] << endl;
    }
}
```

If we have an array of objects of the derived class `Apple`, the following code may crash.

```
// Apple is derived from Fruit

const size_t numberOfApples = 3;

Apple apples[numberOfApples];

printFruits(apples, numberOfApples); // Might crash!
```

Rec. 13.7 Do not use unions.

Unions may seem quite easy to use because they look like classes with the exception that they store only one data member at a time. However, the similarity between classes and unions is treacherous. A union cannot have virtual member functions, base classes, static data members, or data members of any type that has a nontrivial default constructor, copy constructor, destructor, or copy assignment operator. This can make unions very hard to use.

Unions can be an indication of a non–

object-oriented design that is hard to extend. Because a union could store different types of data, the programmer needs a way to tell what is actually stored. If the set of different types of data changes, each piece of code that accesses the object must be rewritten. This disadvantage can be made less serious by putting all access to the union inside a class, instead of putting it directly in many different places in the code.

The usual alternative to unions is inheritance and dynamic binding. The advantage of having a derived class representing each type of value stored is that the set of derived classes can be extended without rewriting any code. Because code with unions is only slightly more efficient, but much more difficult to maintain, you should avoid it unless you have a very good reason.

chapter fourteen

14

Size of Executables

There are many things that can make a program unnecessarily large:

* Unneeded code linked with the program,
* Duplicated program code or data

Too extensive copying of code makes a program hard to maintain and increases the size of the program. Therefore, you should try to reuse code to a large extent.

There is a tradeoff between the size of an executable and its performance. Inline functions can make a program faster, but because many inline functions increase the size of a program, the effect could be the opposite.

Before making a function inline it is necessary to check whether the need for inlining really exists.

RULES AND
RECOMMENDATIONS

Rec. 14.1   Avoid duplicated code and data.

Rule 14.2   When a public base class has a virtual destructor, each derived class should declare and implement a destructor.

See Also

Rec. 7.1: When to make functions `inline`.

Rule 10.4: How to declare destructors for derived classes.

Rec. 14.1 Avoid duplicated code and data.

Large programs can impede the overall performance of a system. If an operating system with multitasking is used, each program must share the CPU with other programs. If the program is large, it is less likely that the program can stay in memory while the operating system runs other programs. More time will be spent in swapping programs in and out of memory because the time for context switches will increase. Reading pages of large programs from memory is time-consuming. This can reduce the amount of actual work that is done by a program during a time slot.

Without proper care when implementing and using classes, many programs could become unnecessarily large.

Reuse of code has the benefit of making a program easier to maintain. An additional benefit is better quality because code that is reused has been tested at least once. In theory, reuse should make a program smaller, but a common problem is that many class libraries give the client a larger executable instead. A problem is that most linkers will link a function even if it is not called by the program. The result is a code bloat that can be avoided only by carefully organizing the source code. The problem could be partially solved by putting each function definition in its own implementation file. Not even this kind of drastic solution is complete because all virtual functions that a program can use must be linked. Because these are called indirectly, the compiler has no way of knowing exactly which ones that are not needed.

All these problems are technical and will probably be solved in the future. Try to reuse code to a large extent; there is good chance that you can get better and smaller programs.

Program size also depends on how different compilers treat inline functions. It is possible to speed up the program by using inline functions, but if these make the program too large, they will slow it down. There is a tradeoff between inlining and program size that must be taken seriously.

The `inline` keyword is a hint to the compiler to inline-expand the function body where the function is called. Inline functions are not meant to be called as ordinary functions, but sometimes the compiler is unable to inline-expand them, and in such cases the compiler generates a function with local linkage that can be called by programs. This generated function is similar to a static function in that it can be called only inside the file that defines it.

Because the generated functions have local linkage, the compiler will generate many copies of the function (one for each implementation file that includes the header file with its definition). The total amount of code generated could become large unless the linker is smart enough to remove excessive copies. Unfortunately, not all linkers are that smart. The general recommendation is therefore to declare functions as `inline` only if they are actually inline-expanded.

Inline-expansion could fail if the inline function contains loops, the address of an inline function is used, or an inline function is called in a complex expression. In some of these cases, the compiler cannot inline-expand the function. The rules for inlining are compiler-dependent, but to be on the safe side, avoid the cases mentioned here.

Constructors and destructors are often too complex for inlining even though they appear to be simple. Do not forget that constructors and destructors for the base class and data members are called implicitly.

Virtual member functions can often be simple enough for inlining, but they should not be declared `inline`.

Rule 14.2 When a public base class has a virtual destructor, each derived class should declare and implement a destructor.

A particularly insidious problem, worth making a special rule for, concerns destructors. Destructors are the only virtual functions that could be generated by the compiler. If a base class declares and implements a virtual destructor and if a derived class does not provide one, the compiler must generate a destructor for the derived class.

A compiler must store the addresses of all virtual member functions, to make it possible to bind their calls dynamically. This includes the destructor. Some compilers use the location of the first virtual member function to decide where to allocate the virtual table (a table that stores addresses of virtual member functions). This is dangerous because there could be many such locations if the destructor is the first virtual member function and it has been generated by the compiler. Some compilers will duplicate the virtual table if there is more than one location. This could significantly increase the size of your program.

You should either avoid making the destructor the first virtual member function or make sure that each derived class declares and implements it. The latter solution is better because it is portable. For example, another compiler could instead use the address of the last virtual member function to determine where to allocate the virtual table.

chapter fifteen

Portability

ISO 9126[1] defines portability as "A set of attributes that bear on the ability of software to be transferred from one environment to another."

The word *environment* is not defined, but can typically be

- The operating system (e.g., Mac-OS, NextStep, Solaris, MS-DOS)
- The hardware platform (e.g., Motorola 68K, PowerPC, Sparc, ix86)
- The compiler, version, and vendor (e.g., Borland, Microsoft, IBM, Watcom)
- The GUI system (e.g., OpenWindows, OSF/Motif, MS Windows, OS2/PM)
- The user's language (e.g., English, Swedish, French)
- A set of presentation formats (e.g., how to display time, currency)

Other aspects of the word *environment* are communications, databases, and different kinds of class libraries.

---

1. International Standard ISO/IEC 9126, Information technology—Software product evaluation—Quality characteristics and guidelines for their use. Reference number ISO/IEC 9126:1991(E).

Portability is an issue to all projects involving multiple environments. In this chapter we concentrate on the portability issues close to the C++ language. Other aspects are also relevant, but are beyond the scope of this book.

General Aspects of Portability

Many aspects of C++ are inherently nonportable. They are called either undefined, unspecified, or implementation-defined parts of the language. Then there are pure extensions that are supplied by particular compiler vendors. You should try to avoid all extensions to C++, but if they are needed, their use must be localized to a few places in the code.

RULES AND RECOMMENDATIONS

Rule 15.1   **Do not depend on undefined, unspecified, or implementation-defined parts of the language.**

Rule 15.2   **Do not depend on extensions to the language or the standard library.**

Rec. 15.3   **Make nonportable code easy to find and replace.**

See Also   Rec. 15.13: Unsupported language features must be treated as similar to language extensions.

Rule 15.1 Do not depend on undefined, unspecified, or implementation-defined parts of the language.

Most nonportable code generally falls into three different categories:

- Implementation-defined behavior
- Unspecified behavior
- Undefined behavior

Implementation-defined behavior means that the code is completely legal C++, but compilers may interpret it differently. However, for each implementation-defined aspect there are only a few different ways in which compilers may differ, and the compiler vendor is required to say in the documentation what their particular compiler does. For example, the implementation defines whether a `char` object can store a negative value.

EXAMPLE 15.1 **Implementation-defined behavior**

```
const char c = -100;

if (c < 0)                 // Implementation-defined behavior
{
    // ...
}
```

Unspecified behavior also means that the code is completely legal C++, but compilers may interpret it differently. The difference between implementation-defined behavior and unspecified behavior is that compiler vendors are not required to describe what their particular compilers do. For example, when you cast an integer to an enum, the resulting enum value may in some cases be unspecified.

EXAMPLE 15.2 **Unspecified behavior**

```
enum BasicAttrType
{
    // ...

    counterGauge    = 0x1000,    //   4096
    counterPeg      = 0x2000,    //   8192
    conterAcc       = 0x3000     // 12288
};

BasicAttrType t  = (BasicAttrType) 10000;
// t has unspecified value
```

Undefined behavior means that code is not correct C++. The standard does not specify what a compiler shall do with such code. It may ignore the problem completely, issue an error, or do something else. For example, it is undefined what happens if you dereference a pointer returned from a request for zero bytes of memory.

EXAMPLE 15.3 **Undefined behavior**

```
char* a = new char[0];
cout << *a << endl;        // Undefined behavior
```

All programs that are intended to be portable must avoid all dependencies on such parts of the language. The problem is that there are very few programmers who know of all these parts of C++. Fortunately, many portability problems are so obscure that they seldom occur. In the rest of this chapter we describe the most common ones.

In general, you should stay within the areas of the language that you know well, and consult a book or the language specification itself if you are doing something new that is likely to be nonportable.

Rule 15.2 Do not depend on extensions to the language or the standard library. Extensions to C++ are sometimes necessary. A fully portable program does not depend on such features, but sometimes, for various reasons, it is necessary to use such extensions to the language. You might need to use macros in order to write portable code.

EXAMPLE 15.4 **Language extension**

An extension provided by many compilers for DOS and MS Windows is far and near pointers. By specifying the type of the pointer you can sometimes generate more efficient code for a segmented architecture such as the 80×86 family of processors.

A near pointer is a 16-bit pointer that can be used to access objects within a 64K segment.

```
char __near* np;
```

A far pointer is a 32-bit pointer that can access any available memory area.

```
char __far* fp;
// sizeof(fp) != sizeof(np)
```

Portable code must use macros to make it possible to remove these nonstandard key words when compiling on other platforms.

```
#ifdef UNIX
#define FAR
// ...
#else
#define FAR _far
#endif

char FAR* fp;  // This will now be OK on a UNIX computer
```

Rec. 15.3 Make nonportable code easy to find and replace. Sometimes you have to write nonportable code. The best solution is to write the code so that a new definition of a macro or a type-def, or the replacement of a file, makes the code work in the new environment. The general trick is to isolate such code as much as possible so that it is easy to find and replace.

EXAMPLE 15.5 **Type of fixed size**

```
#ifdef INT32
typedef int sint32;
#else
typedef long sint32;
#endif

sint32 result = 1234 * 567; // result will not overflow
```

To avoid platform-specific behavior, you must choose a suitable representation for the sint32 typedef. Depending on how large the integral types are, you could choose between an int or a long.

Including Files

There are a few nonportable aspects of file inclusion, such as when to write " " or <>, and what can be inside such include brackets.

RULES AND RECOMMENDATIONS

Rule 15.4   Headers supplied by the implementation should go in <> brackets; all other headers should go in " " quotes.

Rec. 15.5   Do not specify absolute directory names in include directives.

Rec. 15.6   include **file names should always be treated as case-sensitive.**

See Also   Rule 2.1: What to include.

Rule 15.4 Headers supplied by the implementation should go in <> brackets; all other headers should go in " " quotes.

All classes and functions in the C++ standard library require the inclusion of a header before they can be used. A header is usually a source file, but it does not have to be so. You should include only standard headers with <>. What happens if a name not defined by the standard appears within <> is defined by the imple-mentation. All nonstandard header files should be included with

" " quotes to avoid such implementation-defined behavior. Most compilers allow both ways because other standards, such as POSIX, recommend the use of <> for inclusion.

EXAMPLE 15.6   **Good and bad way of including files**

```
// Include only standard header with <>
#include <iostream.h>    /* OK: standard header */
#include <MyFile.hh>     /* NO: nonstandard header */

// include any header with ""
#include "stdlib.h"      /* NO: better to use <> */
#include "MyFile.hh"     /* OK */
```

Rec. 15.5 Do not specify absolute directory names in `include` directives.

You should also avoid using directory names in the include directive, because the implementation defines how files in such circumstances are found. Most modern compilers allow relative path names with / as separators because such names have been standardized outside the C++ standard, as in POSIX. Absolute path names and path names with other separators should always be avoided, however.

The file will be searched for in an implementation-defined list of places. Even if one compiler finds this file there is no guarantee that another compiler will. It is better to specify to the build environment where files may be located because then you do not need to change any `include` directives if you switch to another compiler.

EXAMPLE 15.7   **Directory names in `include` directives**

```
#include "inc/MyFile.hh"      /* Not recommended */
#include "inc\MyFile.hh"      /* Not portable */
#include "/gui/xinterface.h"  /* Not portable */
#include "c:\gui\xinterf.h"   /* Not portable */
```

Rec. 15.6 `include` file names should always be treated as case-sensitive.

Some operating systems, such as DOS, Windows NT, and Vax-VMS, do not have case-sensitive file names. When writing programs to such operating systems, the programmer can include a file in many different ways.

If you are inconsistent, your code will be difficult to port to an environment with case-sensitive file names. Therefore, you should always include a file as if it were case-sensitive. You should look at the documentation for the class if you are uncertain.

EXAMPLE 15.8 **Case-sensitivity of header file name**

```
// Includes the same file on Windows NT, but not on UNIX.

#include <Iostream.h>
#include <iostream.h>
#include <iostream.H>
```

The Size and Layout of Objects

The size and layout of objects is implementation-defined in C++ so that compiler vendors can generate code that is as efficient as possible. This is one of the most powerful aspects of C++, as well as one of the most error-prone ones. A few rules and recommendations are needed in order to steer clear of portability problems.

RULES AND RECOMMENDATIONS

Rule 15.7 Do not make assumptions about the size or layout in memory of an object.

Rule 15.8 Do not cast a pointer to a shorter quantity to a pointer to a longer quantity.

Rec. 15.9 If possible, use plain `int` to store, pass, or return integer values.

Rule 15.10 Make sure all conversions from a value of one type to another of a narrower type do not slice off significant data.

Rec. 15.11 Use `typedef`s or classes to hide the representation of application-specific data types.

See Also Rec. 6.1–Rec. 6.3: How to use casts.

Rec. 7.3–Rec. 7.5: How to pass arguments.

Rule 15.7 Do not make assumptions about the size or layout in memory of an object.

The sizes of built-in types are different in different environments. For example, an `int` may be 16, 32, or even 64 bits long. The layout of objects is also different in different environments, so it is unwise to make any kind of assumption about the layout in memory of objects, such as when lumping together different data in a `struct`.

EXAMPLE 15.9   **Offset of a data member**

```
struct PersonRecord
{
    char         ageM;
    unsigned int phoneNumberM;
    EmcString    nameM;
};
```

A compiler is entitled to significant freedom when laying out such data in memory to find the most efficient solution. The exact address of the `ageM`, `phoneNumberM`, and `nameM` data members within an object of type `PersonRecord` can vary between different environments.

Rule 15.8 Do not cast a pointer to a shorter quantity to a pointer to a longer quantity.

Certain types have alignment requirements, which are requirements about the addresses of objects. For example, some architectures require that objects of a certain size start at an even address. It is a fatal error if a pointer to an object of that size points to an odd address. For example, you might have a `char` pointer and want to convert it to an `int` pointer. If the pointer points to an address that is illegal for an `int`, dereferencing the `int` pointer creates a runtime error.

EXAMPLE 15.10   **Cast must obey alignment rules**

```
int stepAndConvert(const char* a, int n)
{
    const char* b = a + n;  // step n chars ahead
    return *(int*) b;
    // NO: Dangerous cast of const char* to int*
}
```

Calling `stepAndConvert()` will probably create a runtime error for many combinations of the two parameters (a, n).

```
const char data[] = "abcdefghijklmnop";
int anInt = 3;
int i = stepAndConvert(data, anInt);    // NO: May crash
```

This kind of code is unlikely to work, but if it does, it will certainly not be portable.

Rec. 15.9 If possible, use plain int to store, pass, or return integer values.

Plain `int` is the most efficient integral type on most systems because it has the natural word size suggested by the machine architecture. As a rule, fewer machine instructions are needed when you have operands that have the natural word size of the processor. However, there are exceptions, such as the Alpha processor from Digital, which has 32-bit `int`s, 64-bit `long` ints, and a natural word size of 64 bits. However, in most cases, if you select any other type you should have a good reason.

Selecting a `short int` instead of a plain `int` does not make sense unless you are very tight on memory, and a `long int` should be used only if it will hold values so large that plain `int`s are not big enough.

Rule 15.10 Make sure all conversions from a value of one type to another of a narrower type do not slice off significant data.

Converting values from a longer to a narrower type is potentially unsafe because significant data may be lost.

Most compilers warn about dangerous conversions, and you should try to rewrite the code, if necessary, to avoid them. For example, you could use a data type with larger range.

You could also look through your code to see whether such dangerous conversions are possible.

EXAMPLE 15.11   **OS-specific** `typedef`

The Unix system call `fork()` returns a value of a type given by the `typedef pid_t`. Some systems define `pid_t` as a `short`.

```
// fork() returns pid_t that is sometimes a short
short int pid1 = fork(); // NO: should use pid_t
```

If a `typedef` is provided, you should always use it instead of the actual type. In this particular case, we should use `pid_t`.

```
pid_t pid2 = fork();        // Recommended
```

Rec. 15.11 Use typedefs or classes to hide the representation of application-specific data types.

An application-specific type is used to store a quantity that varies between different environments. By providing a `typedef` or a class, the programmer can write more portable code. Such types should be used only when there is a real need for them. `typedefs` make the code more difficult to read, and classes can have negative impact on performance.

Unsupported Language Features

A common problem is using compilers that do not implement all features of the language. By looking forward you can prevent many potential problems.

RULES AND RECOMMENDATIONS

Rec. 15.12   Always prefix global names (such as externally visible classes, functions, variables, constants, `typedefs`, and `enums`) if `namespace` is not supported by the compiler.

Rec. 15.13   Use macros to prevent use of unsupported keywords.

Rec. 15.14   Do not reuse variables declared inside a `for` loop.

See Also

Rec. 1.4: Names that should be put in `namespaces`.

Rule 4.1: How to write a `for` loop.

Rec. 15.12 Always prefix global names (such as externally visible classes, functions, variables, constants, typedefs, and enums) if namespace is not supported by the compiler.

It is possible to avoid name clashes by putting declarations and definitions inside namespaces. Without namespaces, many definitions and declarations will be global. In such cases, you can avoid name clashes by adding a unique prefix to each global name.

Other solutions, such as putting declarations and definitions inside classes as static members, should be avoided unless there is a close relationship between the nested identifier and the class.

EXAMPLE 15.12   **Prefixed name**

```
EmcString famousClimber = "Edmund Hillary";
// Uses Emc as prefix
```

Rec. 15.13 Use macros to prevent use of unsupported keywords. The C++ standard has added many new keywords to the language. The current list contains 62 keywords.

asm	float	static
auto	for	static_cast
bool	friend	struct
break	goto	switch
case	if	template
catch	inline	this
char	int	throw
class	long	true
const	mutable	try
const_cast	namespace	typedef
continue	new	typeid
default	operator	typename
delete	private	union
do	protected	unsigned
double	public	using
dynamic_cast	register	virtual
else	reinterpret _cast	void
enum	return	volatile
explicit	short	wchar_t
extern	signed	while
false	sizeof	

The language also provides textual, alternative representations for some of the operators.

and (&&)	compl (~)	or_eq (|=)
and_eq (&=)	not (!)	xor (^)
bitand (&)	not_eq (!=)	xor_eq (^=)
bitor (|)	or (||)	

None of these names are legal to use as identifiers, but many compilers are not up-to-date with the standard.

EXAMPLE 15.13   **Unsupported keyword as an empty macro**

If your compiler does not support the keyword explicit, which is used to prevent a constructor from defining an implicit conversion, it is useful to define an empty macro with the same name as the keyword.

```
#ifdef NO_EXPLICIT
#define explicit
#endif
```

By doing so, you prevent many potential problems that would result from using the keyword incorrectly.

```
EmcString explicit; // Error: explicit is keyword
// will not compile if explicit defined as macro
```

An additional benefit is that you can use a keyword in places where it is intended to be used.

```
class EmcArray
{
    public:
        explicit EmcArray(size_t size);
        // ...
};
```

However, the macro does not work as the keyword does because it does not stop the constructor from working as an implicit conversion from the type of the parameter to the type of the class. The macro works only as a way for the implementor of the class to tell the user that the constructor should not be used for implicit conversions.

EXAMPLE 15.14   **Forward-compatibility macros**

Here are some other useful macro definitions and typedefs.

```
#ifdef NO_BOOL
typedef int bool;
const bool false = 0;
const bool true  = 1;
#endif
```

```
#ifdef NO_MUTABLE
#define mutable
#endif

#ifdef NO_EXCEPTION
#define throw(E) abort();
#define try
#define catch(T) if (0)
#endif
```

The library standard defines numerous names that should be avoided. Most of them are put inside the namespace std in order to reduce the chance that they will cause trouble. We do not include this list in this book because it contains more than 800 names. It is also unlikely that anyone would want to spend time checking that list while reviewing code.

Rec. 15.14 Do not reuse variables declared inside a for loop.

The scope of a variable declared inside a for statement has been changed by the C++ standard. Previously such a variable belonged to the enclosing scope, but now it belongs to the block following the for statement. This means that a variable declared in a for loop can no longer be reused in the enclosing scope. If you want to reuse a loop variable you need to move the declaration outside the for loop.

EXAMPLE 15.15   Reusing a loop variable

```
int i = 0;

for(; i < last(); i++)
{
    // ...
}

for(; i >= first(); i--)
{
    // ...
}
```

Other Compiler Differences

Some parts of C++ have never been clearly specified. This is particularly true of templates. Such parts of C++ should be handled with care because compilers often handle them differently. The best thing to do is to have a design that is as good as possible and code that can be compiled for the platforms chosen. Another solution is to use only compilers that implement templates the same way, or use only one compiler. If that is not possible, you must either restrict yourself to the parts of the language that are implemented by all compilers or try to make your code easy to modify for new platforms.

RULES AND RECOMMENDATIONS

Rec. 15.15   Only one include directive should be needed when using a template.

Rec. 15.16   Do not rely on partial instantiation of templates.

Rec. 15.17   Do not rely on the lifetime of temporaries.

Rec. 15.18   Do not use `pragma`s.

Rule 15.19   Always return a value from `main()`.

Rec. 15.20   Do not depend on the order of evaluation of arguments to a function.

See Also

Rec. 2.5: How to organize templates.

Rec. 7.3–Rec. 7.5: Argument passing.

Rec. 15.15 Only one include directive should be needed when using a template.

How should you organize your templates?

A template has an interface and an implementation, just as any class or function does. A template is similar to an `inline` function. The compiler must see both the interface and the implementation when code is generated.

A template is automatically instantiated for all template arguments that the program uses. It is also possible to request it to be instantiated for a particular set of arguments. The reason why you would want such explicit instantiations is to reduce the compile time for your program.

EXAMPLE 15.16 **Using a template**

```
// emcMax is function template

template<class T>
const T& emcMax(const T& a, const T& b)
{
    return (a > b) ? a : b;
}

void foo(int i, int j)
{
    int m = emcMax(i, j);    // usage of emcMax<int>
}

EmcQueue<int> q; // usage of class EmcQueue<int> and
                 // EmcQueue<int>:s default constructor

q.insert(42);    // usage of EmcQueue<int>::insert

template class EmcQueue<char>; // Explicit instantiation
```

There is no standard for how template source code is organized and how much of a template to instantiate for a particular set of arguments.

A function template is used when it is called or its address is taken. A class template is used when instances of the class template are used to declare objects.

Some compilers require that the implementation either be part of the header file or be included by the header file. Other compilers use file-name conventions to determine where to find the implementation.

This is a potential portability problem in code using templates. We recommend that you always put the implementation in a separate file, a template definition file. By using conditional compilation to control whether this file is included, you can use the same source code with different compilers.

EXAMPLE 15.17   **Template header file**

By having a macro EXTERNAL_TEMPLATE_DEFINITION, it is possible, at compile time, to control whether the implementation file is included by the header file.

```
template <class T>
class EmcQueue
{
    // ...
};


#ifndef EXTERNAL_TEMPLATE_DEFINITION
#include <EmcQueue.cc>
#endif
```

Rec. 15.16 Do not rely on partial instantiation of templates.

A difference between compilers that is more difficult to handle is the degree of instantiation of a template class.

Some compilers allow a template class to be instantiated for types that do not provide all operators or member functions needed by the implementation. As long as you do not use the part of the implementation that requires these operators or functions, no error is reported by these compilers. This is called partial instantiation.

Other compilers instantiate all members of a template class. Therefore, the template argument must support all uses of the type, even if only a few of the member functions are used. The only solution that always works is to avoid relying on partial instantiation; that is, always assume that all member functions are instantiated.

Rec. 15.17 Do not rely on the lifetime of temporaries.

Temporary objects are often created in C++, such as when a function returns a value or when a parameter to a function is passed by a value. The lifetime of temporaries was implementation-defined for a long time, but it has now been decided that they must persist at least until the end of the full expression in which they were created. Unfortunately, your compiler still might not implement that behavior. Therefore, you should take great care not to depend on the lifetime of temporaries.

EXAMPLE 15.18 Temporary objects

Temporary objects are often created when operating on objects that store values such as strings. If the class also provides a conversion operator that returns a pointer or reference to the representation, then you have potentially dangerous code.

```
class DangerousString
{
   public:
      DangerousString(const char* cp);
      operator const char*() const;
      // conversion operator gives access to data member
      // ...
};
```

The conversion operator to `const char*` is used to access the representation of the string so that it can be printed by calling `ostream::operator<<(const char*)`. The problem with this is that the `DangerousString` object to be printed could be a temporary (for example, one that stores the result of an expression). Because the lifetimes of those objects vary between implementations, there is a risk that the pointer might become invalid before it is used.

```
DangerousString operator+(const DangerousString& left,
                          const DangerousString& right);

DangerousString a = "This may go";
DangerousString b = " wrong";
cout << a << endl;          // OK
cout << a + b << endl;      // Dangerous
```

The solution in this particular case is to add an output operator for `DangerousString` objects. Because a reference to the temporary is passed to the function, the compiler must guarantee that the object bound to that reference exists until the function returns.

```
ostream&
   operator<<(ostream& o, const DangerousString& s);
```

Rec. 15.18 Do not use
pragmas.

A `pragma` is usually a way to control the compilation process, such as by disabling optimization of a particular function, or to force an inline function to become inline in cases when the compiler normally would refuse to make it inline.

Everything about `pragmas` is implementation-defined, so they are perhaps the most nonportable feature of C++. The preprocessor will handle them if it can understand them; otherwise they will just be ignored. You cannot be completely sure a new compiler will understand any `pragmas` in your code.

It is OK to use `pragmas` only as long as your code will work correctly without them. Therefore, you should use them sparingly and always document why and where they are used.

EXAMPLE 15.19   **A `pragma` directive**

The pragma `once` was previously provided by the g++ compiler as a way for the programmer to tell the preprocessor which files are `include` files. Files with the `pragma` should be included only once.

```
#pragma once   /* NO: not portable! */
```

Rule 15.19 Always
return a value from
`main()`.

The standardization committee for C++ has decided that the return values of functions must always be declared. Functions without return values were previously assumed to return an `int`. Therefore you now have to declare `main` to return an `int`, and you should also always return a value. This is good because in many environments this return value is checked by other programs.

EXAMPLE 15.20   **How to declare `main()`**

```
int main()              // Yes
{
    // ...
    return 0;           // Yes
}
```

Rec. 15.20 Do not
depend on the order of
evaluation of arguments
to a function.

Another area where compilers differ is the order of evaluation of function arguments.

EXAMPLE 15.21   Evaluation order of arguments

```
func(f1(), f2(), f3());
// f1 may be evaluated before f2 and f3,
// but don't depend on it!
```

The order of evaluation of expressions that are part of a larger expression is in many cases unspecified. A portable program should not depend on any specific order.

EXAMPLE 15.22   Evaluation order of subexpressions

```
a[i++] = i;   // NO: i may be incremented before or
              // after its value is used on the right
              // side of the assignment.
```

appendix
A

Style

Code is always written in a particular style. Naming conventions, file-name extensions, and lexical style are all part of this structure we call *style*. Discussing style is highly controversial, which is why we have placed it in an appendix, to keep it distinct from all other rules and recommendations.

General Aspects of Style

The most important aspect of style, whatever style you use, is to be consistent.

RULES AND RECOMMENDATIONS

Style A.1 Do not mix coding styles with in a group of closely related classes.

Style A.1   **Do not mix coding styles with in a group of closely related classes.**

For each project, or group of closely related classes, you should select a coding style. Code written by one programmer might be maintained by another, so the same style should be used by all programmers on the project. If you modify files from another project, you should stick to the style chosen for that project.

However, sometimes you may be forced to mix code written with different styles. For example, it could be code reused from

183

previous projects using a different style than the one chosen for your project, from third-party libraries, or from the standard library. In such cases you can select the style used by the standard library, the style used by the third-party library, a combination of the two styles, or the style described in this appendix. You might deliberately use different styles for different kinds of code, but there are obvious reasons for having the same style for all code in the whole project. Mixing libraries is very common, which means that style issues are bound to be a problem, but mixing styles within a group of closely related classes is likely to be very confusing, and should therefore be avoided if possible.

It should be noted that the standard library uses a style that in some cases is different from what we recommend, particularly in how class names are written. It is our belief that this will cause little confusion because the names and usage of the components in the standard library are known and used by all programmers and thus are easily distinguished from code written by users in a project.

Naming Conventions

Along with the issue of selecting good names for the abstractions in a program is the question of how these names should be written. Should you use uppercase or lowercase characters? How should names consisting of many words be written? In this section we present one such naming style.

RULES AND RECOMMENDATIONS

Style A.2	In names that consist of more than one word, the words are written together and each word other than the first begins with an uppercase letter.
Style A.3	The names of classes, `typedefs`, and enumerated types should begin with uppercase letters.
Style A.4	The names of variables and functions should begin with lowercase letters.
Style A.5	Let data members have an *M* as a suffix.
Style A.6	The names of macros should be uppercase.
Style A.7	The name of an `include` guard should be the name of the header file, with all illegal characters replaced by underscores and all letters converted to uppercase.

Style A.8   Do not use letters that can be mistaken for digits, and vice versa.

Style A.2 In names that consist of more than one word, the words are written together and each word other than the first begins with an uppercase letter.

There are a few different ways to separate words in identifiers. One is to use underscores and another is to let the first letter in each new word be in uppercase. We have chosen the latter approach because such identifiers are shorter and easier to read. Both naming conventions have their pros and cons.

EXAMPLE A.1   **How to separate words in an identifier**

```
int max_timeout_time = 1000;     // Not recommended
int maxTimeOutTime = 1000;       // Recommended
```

Style A.3 The names of classes, `typedefs`, and enumerated types should begin with uppercase letters.

Style A.4 The names of variables and functions should begin with lowercase letters.

Type names, like classes and enumerated types, should always begin with an uppercase letter to distinguish them from variables and functions, which should begin with a lowercase letter.

EXAMPLE A.2   **Naming style**

```
class Browser;                    // Class
enum State { green, yellow, red }; // Enum
int n = 0;                        // Local variables
void Browser::show()              // Member function
{
    // ...
};
```

Style A.5 Let data members have an M as a suffix.

It is useful to have a naming convention that clearly distinguishes data members from local variables, function parameters, and member functions. We suggest adding an M (as in *Member*) as a suffix to data members. The implementation of member functions is easier to understand if data members are easy to distinguish in the code.

EXAMPLE A.3   **Data member suffix**

```
template<class T>
class EmcStack
{
   public:
      // ...
   private:
      unsigned allocatedM;
      T*        vectorM;
      int       topM;
};
```

Style A.6 The names of
macros should be
uppercase.

Names in uppercase letters are reserved for macros. This is the
traditional naming convention for macros, and we think it is a
good idea to keep this tradition. However, macros should be quite
unusual in C++ because const variables, enum values, and inline
functions often are better and safer alternatives to macros.

EXAMPLE A.4   **Names of macros**

```
#define SQUARE(x) (x)*(x)        /* Recommended name */
```

Style A.7 The name of
an include guard
should be the name of
the header file, with all
illegal characters
replaced by underscores
and all letters converted
to uppercase.

include guards are macros, and as such they should also be in
uppercase letters. We suggest that the name of an include guard
should be the name of the header file, with all illegal characters
replaced by underscores and all letters converted to uppercase.

It is important to have a consistent style for the names of these
macros because that will save programmers from having to look in
the header file to know the name of the include guard. The file
name should be enough to deduce the name of the include guard.

EXAMPLE A.5   **Names of** include **guards**

```
// In file File.hh
#ifndef FILE_HH
#define FILE_HH

// The rest of the file

#endif /* FILE_HH */
```

Style A.8 Do not use letters that can be mistaken for digits, and vice versa.

Some digits are rather similar to some letters. The digit 0 is similar to the letter O, 1 is similar to l, and 5 is similar to S. They are often mistaken for each other, which can be confusing.

EXAMPLE A.6 **Integral suffixes**

A suffix can be used to specify the type of an integer value. You can use either L or l if the value is a `long int`, but the lowercase l should be avoided because it can be mistaken for the digit 1.

```
long i1 = 1l;  // Not recommended
long i2 = 1L;  // Better
```

File-Name Extensions

A convention for choosing file-name extensions will make it easy for tools and users to distinguish between different types of files.

RULES AND RECOMMENDATIONS

Style A.9   Header files should have the extension .hh.

Style A.10   Inline definition files should have the extension .icc.

See Also   Rec. 2.4: What to put in inline definition file.

Style A.9 Header files should have the extension .hh.

Style A.10 Inline definition files should have the extension .icc.

There are many different file name extensions in use. This is a list of some of them:

Header files	.h, .hh, .H, .hpp, .hxx
Implementation files	.c, .cc, .C, .cpp, .cxx, .cp
Inline definition files	.icc, .i

Here, we only have recommendations for header files and inline definition files. Using only one extension standard for implementation files helps, but for practical reasons, it is often necessary to have different extensions for different platforms. Some compilers do not recognize files with certain extensions; furthermore, they do not allow you to override which suffixes they recognize, forcing you to use some other extension instead. Fortunately, this is particularly important because client code should normally not depend on the name extensions for implementation files.

We have chosen to avoid the extensions .h and .c because they are used by the C standard. We have also avoided all extensions with uppercase letters, such as .H and .C, because some operating systems do not distinguish mixed-case file names. Of the remaining ones, we prefer .hh, .icc, and .cc, but for reasons mentioned above we only have recommendations for .hh and .icc.

Lexical Style

A lexical style is a preferred way to combine the lexical tokens of the language. Such a style should be chosen to avoid having code that is difficult to read and understand just because different parts of it look different.

RULES AND RECOMMENDATIONS

Style A.11   The names of parameters to functions should be specified in the function declaration if the type name is insufficient to describe the parameter.

Style A.12   Always provide an access specifier for base classes and data members.

Style A.13   The public, protected, and private sections of a class should be declared in that order.

Style A.14   The keyword `struct` should be used only for a C-style struct.

Style A.15   Define inline member functions outside the class definition.

Style A.16   Write unary operators together with their operands.

Style A.17   Write access operators together with their operands.

Style A.18   Do not access static members with `.` or `->`.

Style A.11 The names of parameters to functions should be specified in the function declaration if the type name is insufficient to describe the parameter.

The declaration of a function often contains more information than the compiler needs to see. For example, names of formal parameters are needed only in the function definition, not in declarations.

Parameter names are meant to make it easier for a programmer to understand the purpose and use of a function. It is generally better to supply too many names than too few, but if the type name is sufficient to describe the purpose of a parameter, the declaration will be shorter and as easy to understand as without the name.

EXAMPLE A.7   **Specifying parameter names**

Let's take a look at the `list` class in the standard library.

```
template<class T>
class list
{
    public:
        list();
        explicit list(const T&);
        list(const list<T>&);
        list<T>& operator=(const list<T>&);
        ~list();
        // member template
        template <class InputIterator>
        void insert(iterator position,
                    InputIterator first,
                    InputIterator last);
        void insertFirst(const T&);
        void insertLast(const T&);
        // ...
};
```

The purpose of all member functions above is obvious from their names and the type of the parameters, except for the only member function with two parameters of the same type, the `insert()` member function. To explain the purpose of each parameter, all of them have been given names.

Style A.12 Always provide an access specifier for base classes and data members.

All members of a class are private unless the class has an access specification. Likewise, a base class is private unless declared otherwise. You should not use this default behavior. It is much better to explicitly show the reader of the code what you mean.

EXAMPLE A.8   **Implicitly given access specifiers**

```
// Base class B implicitly declared private

class A : B            // Not recommended
{
        // Not recommended: implicit access specifier
        int i;
    public:
        // ...
};
```

EXAMPLE A.9   Explicitly given access specifiers

```
// Base class B explicitly declared private

class A : private B  // Recommended
{
   public:
      // ...

   private:   // Recommended: explicit access specifier
      int i;
};
```

Style A.13 The public, protected, and private sections of a class should be declared in that order.

The public part should be most interesting to the user of the class, and should therefore come first. The protected part is of interest to derived classes and should therefore come after the public part, and the private part should be of no interest to the user and should therefore be listed last in the class declaration.

Style A.14 The keyword struct should be used only for a C-style struct.

There is only one major difference between a struct and a class in C++: Everything in a struct is public by default, which is different from a class, where everything is private by default. This is for compatibility with C, because everything in a C struct is public. Apart from that, there are no big differences. A struct can have member functions and inherit from other classes. It would be possible to use only structs instead of classes, but that would make your code more difficult to understand.

To avoid confusion, the keyword struct should be used only when you are grouping built-in data types into a C-style struct, or POD-struct (POD is an acronym for *plain old data*). A struct should therefore have no member functions or data members of class types. In other words, if you group anything in a struct that does not exist in C (such as references or class objects) you should use a class instead.

Style A.15 Define inline member functions outside the class definition.

Inline member functions can be defined inside or outside the class definition. We strongly recommend the second alternative. The class definition will be more compact and comprehensible if no implementation can be seen in the class interface.

EXAMPLE A.10   **Where to implement inline member functions**

```
class X
{
    public:
        // Not recommended: function definition in class
        bool insideClass() const { return false; }
        bool outsideClass() const;
};


// Recommended: function definition outside class
inline bool X::outsideClass() const
{
    return true;
}
```

Style A.16 Write unary operators together with their operands.

The various operators should be presented to the reader so that their use is completely clear. Some of them look identical but are very different, such as unary and binary *. Unary operators such as unary * and ++ are best written together with their operands.

EXAMPLE A.11   **How to write unary operators**

```
int* i = new int(77);

cout << * i << endl;      // Not recommended
cout << *i << endl;       // Recommended
```

Style A.17 Write access operators together with their operands.

Access operators, such as . and ->, are best written together with their operands.

EXAMPLE A.12   **How to write access operators**

```
a->foo();          // Recommended
b.bar();           // Recommended
```

Style A.18 Do not access static members with . or ->.

Static members are members of the class, not of an object of the class. Accessing such members as if they were object members would therefore be confusing.

EXAMPLE A.13 **How to access static members**

```
class G
{
   public:
      // ...
      static G* create();
      // ...
};

G* G::create()
{
   return new G;
}

G g;
G* gp = new G;
G* gp1 = g.create();      // Not recommended
G* gp2 = gp->create();    // Not recommended
G* gp3 = G::create();     // Recommended
```

appendix B

Terminology

The terminology used by this book is as defined by the "Draft Standard for the Programming Language C++," with some additions presented below.

ABSTRACT BASE CLASS   An **abstract base class** is a class with at least one pure virtual member function.

ACCESS FUNCTION
ACCESSOR   An **access function (accessor)** is a member function that returns a value and that does not modify the object's state.

BUILT-IN TYPE   A **built-in type** is one of the types defined by the language, such as int, short, char, and bool.

CLASS INVARIANT   A **class invariant** is a condition that defines all valid states for an object. An class invariant is both a precondition and post-condition to a member function of the class.

CONST CORRECT   A program is const **correct** if it has correctly declared functions, parameters, return values, variables, and member functions as const.

COPY ASSIGNMENT
OPERATOR   The **copy assignment operator** of a class is the assignment operator that takes a reference to an object of the same class as a parameter.

COPY CONSTRUCTOR	The **copy constructor** of a class is the constructor that takes a reference to an object of the same class as a parameter.
DANGLING POINTER	A **dangling pointer** points at an object that has been deleted.
DECLARATIVE REGION	A **declarative region** is the largest part of a program where a name declared can be used with its unqualified name.
DIRECT BASE CLASS	The **direct base class** of a class is the class explicitly mentioned as a base class in its definition. All other base classes are **indirect base classes**.
DYNAMIC BINDING	A member function call is **dynamically bound** if different functions will be called depending on the type of the object operated on.
ENCAPSULATION	**Encapsulation** allows a user to depend only on the class interface, and not upon its implementation.
EXCEPTION SAFE	A class is **exception safe** if its objects do not lose any resources, and do not invalidate their class invariant or terminate the application when they end their lifetimes because of an exception.
EXPLICIT TYPE CONVERSION	An **explicit type conversion** is the conversion of an object from one type to another where you explicitly write the resulting type.
FILE SCOPE	An object with **file scope** is accessible only to functions within the same translation unit.
FLOW CONTROL PRIMITIVE	The **flow control primitives** are `if-else`, `switch`, `do-while`, `while`, and `for`.
FORWARDING FUNCTION	A **forwarding function** is a function that does nothing more than call another function.
FREE STORE	An object on the **free store** is an object allocated with `new`.
GLOBAL OBJECT	A **global object** is an object in global scope.
GLOBAL SCOPE	An object or type is in **global scope** if it can be accessed from within any function of a program.
IMPLEMENTATION-DEFINED BEHAVIOR	Code with **implementation-defined behavior** is completely legal C++, but compilers may differ. Compiler vendors are required to describe what their particular compiler does with such code.

IMPLICIT TYPE CONVERSION	An **implicit type conversion** occurs when an object is converted from one type to another and when you do not explicitly write the resulting type.
INHERITANCE	A derived class **inherits** state and behavior from a base class.
INLINE DEFINITION FILE	An **inline definition file** is a file that contains only definitions of inline functions.
ITERATOR	An **iterator** is an object used to traverse through collections of objects.
LITERAL	A **literal** is a sequence of digits or characters that represents a constant value.
MEMBER OBJECT	The **member objects** of a class are its base classes and data members.
MODIFYING FUNCTION (MODIFIER)	A **modifying function** (**modifier**) is a member function that changes the value of at least one data member.
NONCOPYABLE CLASS	A class is **noncopyable** if its objects cannot be copied.
OBJECT-ORIENTED PROGRAMMING	A language supports **object-oriented programming** if it provides encapsulation, inheritance, and polymorphism.
POLYMORPHISM	**Polymorphism** means that an expression can have many different interpretations depending on the context. This means that the same piece of code can be used to operate on many types of objects, as provided by dynamic binding and parameterization, for example.
POSTCONDITION	A **postcondition** is a condition that must be true on exit from a member function if the precondition was valid on entry to that function. A class is implemented correctly if postconditions are never false.
PRECONDITION	A **precondition** is a condition that must be true on entry to a member function. A class is used correctly if preconditions are never false.
RESOURCE	A **resource** is something that more than one program needs, but of which there is limited availability. Resources can be acquired and released.

SELF-CONTAINED   A header file is **self-contained** if nothing more than its inclusion is needed to use the full interface of a class.

SIGNATURE   The **signature** of a function is defined by its return type, its parameter types and their order, and whether it has been declared `const` or volatile.

SLICING   **Slicing** means that the data added by a subclass are discarded when an object of the subclass is passed or returned by value to or from a function expecting a base class object.

STACK UNWINDING   **Stack unwinding** is the process during exception handling when the destructor is called for all local objects between the place where the exception was thrown and where it is caught.

STATE   The **state** of an object is the data members of the object, and possibly also other data to which the object has access, which affects the observable behavior of the object.

SUBSTITUTABILITY   **Substitutability** means that it is possible to use a pointer or reference to an object of a derived class wherever a pointer or reference to an object of a public base class is used.

TEMPLATE DEFINITION FILE   A **template definition file** is a file containing only definitions of non-inline template functions.

TRANSLATION UNIT   A **translation unit** is the result of merging an implementation file with all its headers and header files.

UNDEFINED BEHAVIOR   Code with **undefined behavior** is not correct C++. The standard does not specify what a compiler should do with such code. It may ignore the problem completely, issue an error, or do something else.

UNSPECIFIED BEHAVIOR   Code with **unspecified behavior** is completely legal C++, but compilers may differ. Compiler vendors are not required to describe what their particular compiler does with such code.

USER-DEFINED CONVERSION   A **user-defined conversion** is a conversion from one type to another introduced by a programmer; that is, it is not one of the conversions defined by the language. Such user-defined conversions are either nonexplicit constructors taking only one parameter, or conversion operators.

VIRTUAL TABLE   A **virtual table** is an array of pointers to all virtual member functions of a class. Many compilers generate such tables to implement dynamic binding of virtual functions.

Rules and Recommendations

Chapter 1 Naming

Meaningful Names

Rec. 1.1 Use meaningful names

Rec. 1.2 Use English names for identifiers.

Rec. 1.3 Be consistent when naming functions, types, variables, and constants.

Names That Collide

Rec. 1.4 Only `namespace` names should be global.

Rec. 1.5 Do not use global `using` declarations and `using` directives inside header files.

Rec. 1.6 Prefixes should be used to group macros.

Rec. 1.7 Group related files by using a common prefix in the file name.

Illegal Naming

Rule 1.8 Do not use identifiers that contain two or more underscores in a row.

Rule 1.9 Do not use identifiers that begin with an underscore.

Chapter 2 Organizing the Code

Rule 2.1 Each header file should be self-contained.

Rule 2.2 Avoid unnecessary inclusion.

Rule 2.3 Enclose all code in header files within `include` guards.

Rec. 2.4 Definitions for inline member functions should be placed in a separate file.

Rec. 2.5 Definitions for all template functions of a class should be placed in a separate file.

Chapter 3 Comments

Rec. 3.1 Each file should contain a copyright comment.

Rec. 3.2 Each file should contain a comment with a short description of the file content.

Rec. 3.3 Every file should declare a local constant string that identifies the file.

Rec. 3.4 Use // for comments.

Rec. 3.5 All comments should be written in English.

Chapter 3 Control Flow

Rule 4.1 Do not change a loop variable inside a for loop block.

Rec. 4.2 Update loop variables close to where the loop condition is specified.

Rec. 4.3 All flow control primitives (if, else, while, for, do, switch, and case) should be followed by a block, even if it is empty.

Rec. 4.4 Statements following a case label should be terminated by a statement that exits the switch statement.

Rec. 4.5 All switch statements should have a default clause.

Rule 4.6 Use break and continue instead of goto.

Rec. 4.7 Do not have overly complex functions.

Chapter 4 Object Life Cycle

Initialization of Variables and Constants

Rec. 5.1 Declare and initialize variables close to where they are used.

Rec. 5.2 If possible, initialize variables at the point of declaration.

Rec. 5.3 Declare each variable in a separate declaration statement.

Rec. 5.4 Literals should be used only in the definition of constants and enumerations.

Constructor Initializer Lists

Rec. 5.5 Initialize all data members.

Rule 5.6 Let the order in the initializer list be the same as the order of declaration in the header file: first base classes, then data members.

Rec. 5.7 Do not use or pass this in constructor initializer lists.

Copying of Objects

Rec. 5.8 Avoid unnecessary copying of objects that are costly to copy.

Rule 5.9 A function must never return, or in any other way give access to, reference or pointers to local variables outside the scope in which they are declared.

Rec. 5.10 If objects of a class should never be copied, then the copy constructor and the copy assignment operator should be declared `private` and not implemented.

Rec. 5.11 A class that manages resources should declare a copy constructor, a copy assignment operator, and a destructor.

Rule 5.12 Copy assignment operators should be protected from doing destructive actions if an object is assigned to itself.

Chapter 6 Conversions

Rec. 6.1 Use explicit rather than implicit type conversions.

Rec. 6.2 Use the new cast operators (`dynamic_cast`, `const_cast`, `reinterpret_cast`, and `static_cast`) instead of the old-style casts, unless portability is an issue.

Rec. 6.3 Do not cast away `const`.

Rule 6.4 Declare a data member `mutable` if it must be modified by a `const` member function.

Chapter 7   The Class Interface

Inline Functions

Rec.   7.1   Make simple functions inline.

Rule   7.2   Do not declare virtual member functions as inline.

Argument Passing and Return Values

Rec.   7.3   Pass arguments of built-in types by value unless the function should modify them.

Red.   7.4   Use a parameter of pointer type only if the function stores the address or passes it to a function that does.

Rec.   7.5   Pass arguments of class types by reference or pointer.

Rule   7.6   Pass arguments of class types by reference or pointer if the class is meant as a public base class.

Rule   7.7   The copy assignment operator should return a non-`const` reference to the object assigned to.

`const` Correctness

Rule   7.8   A pointer or reference parameter should be declared `const` if the function does not change the object bound to it.

Rule   7.9   The copy constructor and copy assignment operator should always have a `const` reference as a parameter.

Rule   7.10   Use only `const char`-pointers to access string literals.

Rule   7.11   A member function that does not change the state of the program should be declared `const`

Rule   7.12   A member function that gives non-`const` access to the representation of an object must not be declared `const`.

Rec.   7.13   Do not let `const` member functions change the state of the program.

Overloading and Default Arguments

Rule   7.14   All variants of an overloaded member function should be used for the same purpose and have similar behavior.

Rec.   7.15   If you overload one out of a closely-related set of operators, then you should overload the whole set and preserve the same invariants that exist for built-in types.

Rule   7.16   In a derived class, if you need to override one of a set of the base classõs overloaded virtual member functions, then you should override the whole set, or use using-declarations to bring all of the functions in the base class into the scope of the derived class.

Rule   7.17   Supply default arguments with the functionõs declaration in the header file, not with the functionõs definition in the implementation file.

Conversion Functions

Rec.   7.18   One-argument constructors should be declared `explicit`.

Rec.   7.19   Do not use conversion functions.

Chapter 8   `new` **and** `delete`

Rule   8.1   `delete` should be used only with `new`.

Rule   8.2   `delete []` should be used only with `new []`.

Rule   8.3   Do not access a pointer or reference to a deleted object.

Rec.   8.4   Do not delete `this`.

Rec.   8.5   If you overload `operator new` for a class, you should have a corresponding overloaded `operator delete`.

Rec.   8.6   Customize the memory management for a class if memory management is an unacceptably large part of the allocation and deallocation of free store objects of that class.

Chapter 9   **Static Objects**

Rec.   9.1   Objects with static storage duration should be declared only within the scope of a class, function, or anonymous namespace.

Rec.   9.2   Document how static objects are initialized.

Chapter 10   Object-Oriented Programming

Encapsulation

Rule   10.1   Declare data members private.

Rec.   10.2   If a member function returns a pointer or reference, you should document how it should be used and for how long it is valid.

Dynamic Binding

Rec.   10.3   Selection statements (`if-else` and `switch`) should be used when the control flow depends on an objectõs value; dynamic binding should be used when the control flow depends on the objectõs type.

Inheritance

Rule   10.4   A public base class must have either a public virtual destructor or a protected destructor.

Rule   10.5   If you derive from more than one base class with the same parent, that parent should be a virtual base class.

The Class Interface

Rec.   10.6   Specify classes using precondition, postconditions, exceptions, and class invariants.

Rec.   10.7   Use C++ to describe preconditions, postconditions, exceptions, and class invariants.

Rec.   10.8   It should be possible to use a pointer or reference to an object of a derived class wherever pointer or reference to a public base class object is used.

Rec.   10.9   Document the interface of template parameters.

Chapter 11   Assertions

Rule   11.1   Do not let assertions change the state of the program.

Rec.   11.2   Remove all assertions from production code.

Chapter 12   Error Handling

Different Ways to Report Errors

Rec.   12.1   Check for all errors reported from functions.

Rec.   12.2   Use exception handling instead of status values and error codes.

When to Throw Exceptions

Rec.   12.3   Throw exceptions only when a function fails to do what it is expected to do.

Rec.   12.4   Do not throw exceptions as a way of reporting uncommon values from a function.

Rule   12.5   Do not let destructors called during stack unwinding throw exceptions.

Rec.   12.6   Constructors of types thrown as exceptions should not themselves throw exceptions.

Exception Safe Code

Rec.   12.7   Use objects to manage resources.

Rule   12.8   A resource managed by an object must be released by the objectõs destructor.

Rec.   12.9   Use stack objects instead of free store objects.

Rec.   12.10   Before letting any exceptions propagate out of a member function, make certain that the class invariant holds and, if possible, leave the state of the object unchanged.

Exception Types

Rec.   12.11   Throw only objects of class type.

Rec.   12.12   Group related exception types by using inheritance.

Rec.   12.13   Catch only objects by reference.

Error Recovery

Rule   12.14   Always catch exceptions the user is not supposed to know about.

Rec.   12.15   Do not catch exceptions your are not supposed to know about.

Exception Specifications

Rec.   12.16   Use exception specifications to declare which exceptions might be thrown from a function.

Chapter 13   Parts of C++ to Avoid

Library Functions to Avoid

Rec.   13.1   Use `new` and `delete` instead of `malloc`, `calloc`, `realloc`, and `free`.

Rule   13.2   Use the `iostream` library instead of C-style I/O.

Rule   13.3   Do not use `setjmp ()` and `longjmp ()`.

Rec.   13.4   Use overloaded functions and chained function calls instead of functions with an unspecified number of arguments.

Language Constructs to Avoid

Rule   13.5   Do not use macros instead of constants, `enums`, functions, or type definitions.

Rec.   13.6   Use an array class instead of built-in arrays.

Rec.   13.7   Do not use unions.

Chapter 14   Size of Executables

Rec.   14.1   Avoid duplicated code and data.

Rule   14.2   When a public base class has a virtual destructor, each derived class has a virtual destructor.

Chapter 15   Portability

General Aspects of Portability

Rule   15.1   Do not depend on undefined, unspecified, or implementation-defined parts of the language.

Rule   15.2   Do not depend on extensions to the language or the standard library.

Rec.   15.3   Make nonportable code easy to find an replace.

Including Files

Rule   15.4   Headers supplied by the implementation should go in `<>` brackets; all other headers should go in `" "` quotes.

Rec.   15.5   Do not specify absolute directory names in `include` directives.

Rec.   15.6   `include` file names should always be treated as case-sensitive.

The Size and Layout of Objects

Rule   15.7   Do not make assumptions about the size or layout in memory of an object.

Rule   15.8   Do not cast a pointer to a shorter quantity to a pointer to a longer quantity.

Rec.   15.9   If possible, use plain `int` to store, pass, or return integer values.

Rule   15.10   Make sure all conversions from a value of one type to another of a narrower type do not slice off significant data.

Rec.   15.11   Use `typedefs` or classes to hide the representation of application-specific data types.

Unsupported Language Features

Rec.   15.12   Always prefix global names (such as externally visible classes, functions, variables, constants, `typedefs`, and `enums`) if `namespace` is not supported by the compiler.

Rec.   15.13   Use macros to prevent use of unsupported key words.

Rec.   15.14   Do not reuse variables declared inside a `for` loop.

Other Compiler Differences

Rec.   15.15   Only one `include` directive should be needed when using a template.

Rec.   15.16   Do not rely on partial instantiation of templates.

Rec.   15.17   Do not rely on the lifetime of temporaries.

Rec.   15.18   Do not use `pragmas`.

Rule   15.19   Always return a value from `main()`.

Rec.   15.20   Do not depend on the order of evaluation of arguments to a function.

Appendix A   Style

General Aspects of Style

Style   A.1   Do not mix coding styles within a group of closely related classes.

Naming Conventions

Style	A.2	In names that consist of more than one word, the words are written together and each word other than the first begins with an uppercase letter.
Style	A.3	The names of classes, `typedefs`, and enumerated types should begin with uppercase letters.
Style	A.4	The names of variables and functions should begin with lowercase letters.
Style	A.5	Let data members have an *M* as a suffix.
Style	A.6	The names of macros should be uppercase.
Style	A.7	The name of an `include` guard should be the name of the header file, with all illegal characters replaced by underscores and all letters converted to uppercase.
Style	A.8	Do not use letters that can be mistaken for digits, and vice versa.

File-Name Extensions

Style	A.9	Header files should have the extension `.hh`.
Style	A.10	Inline definition files should have the extension `.icc`.

Lexical Style

Style	A.11	The names of parameters to functions should be specified in the function declaration if the type name is insufficient to describe the parameter.
Style	A.12	Always provide an access specifier for base classes and data members.
Style	A.13	The public, protected, and private sections of a class should be declared in that order.
Style	A.14	The keyword `struct` should be used only for a C-style struct.
Style	A.15	Define inline member functions outside the class definition.
Style	A.16	Write unary operators together with their operands.
Style	A.17	Write access operators together with their operands.
Style	A.18	Do not access static members with `.` or `->`.

Index